O[ ]CH

How to Bring Back the Exciting Life of the First Century Church

by
James H. Rutz

The SeedSowers

The cover design uses a lion, not as a symbol of Christ, but as a symbol of the strong male lay leaders created in open churches. The towering flame symbolizes God. In this Christian version of a Salvador Dali landscape, the usual image of solid walls enclosing a space is reversed. The vast space swallows up the walls and turns them into floating, near-invisible forms that point toward God's glory.

Published by The SeedSowers, Box 3568, Beaumont, TX, 77704-3568
ISBN **0-940232-50-2**
Library of Congress Catalog Number **92-81563**

PRINTED IN THE UNITED STATES OF AMERICA

First Edition: June, 1992,
Second Edition: February, 1993

ACKNOWLEDGMENTS

Grateful appreciation is extended to the following for permission to quote from their copyrighted materials:

Regal Books. For quote from *Body Life*, by Ray Stedman. © 1979 by Regal Books.

The International Bible Society. For Scriptures from *The New International Version*. © 1978 by The International Bible Society

Dedication: To You

"Then what is the right course, brothers? Whenever [the whole church] meets for worship, *each one* has something to contribute: a song, a piece of teaching, some special information God has given him, a message in an unknown language or an explanation of what it means."

—I Corinthians 14:26 [and 23]

Summary

The unique position of this book is that today's church can regain the quality and dynamics of the early church without abandoning its facilities or staff. The key is to enable everyone to be a participant, not just a spectator. The church can quickly be restored to everyone because, contrary to popular belief, laymen are eager to share their hearts, take active roles in worship, and resume the work of God.

CONTENTS

Forewords

Yes, it still works! Jim Rutz calls us back to the lost dynamic of the early church. You won't be sorry if you try it .

> Dr. Ray C. Stedman
> Author of *Body Life,*
> *Talking to My Father, From Guilt to Glory*
> Former Pastor, Peninsula Bible Church

We have spent the last 2,000 years complicating Christianity. Jim Rutz dares to call us back to church life that more clearly resembles our New Testament model.

> James W. Hayford, Sr.
> The Foursquare Church, Santa Barbara, California
> Author of *Contending for the Authentic*

Ever Feel Like Quitting Church?

If you've ever felt alone and unimportant in church, there's a good reason: You <u>are</u> alone and unimportant.

From 11 to 12 Sunday, you're just another pretty face in the crowd.

Though surrounded by others, you're cut off. Custom walls you off in your own space and silences your voice—except for song or responsive reading.

Surrounded by an audience of trainee mutes, you can find it lonely as a solo trek across Antarctica. After you've eaten all the sled dogs.

The service would be exactly the same without you. You know that. Your impact on it is like an extra gallon of water going over Niagara Falls.

What's wrong here?

The heart of your church is the Sunday service, where the typical communication pattern is about as useful as a jello telephone.

No matter what you have on your heart—the greatest joy or deepest sorrow—you are not allowed to share it during the service. Ever.

Fellowship is confined to the foyer afterward, please. (Unless you've figured a way to fellowship with the back of someone else's head.) Try to talk, and the ushers will ush you out. Post hastily.

This, my friend, is *not* Biblical. Saint Peter would have wept.

In fact, many of the early churches almost *demanded* you share something every week. They even expected you to *sing* for them (aaugh!) Even <u>solos!</u>

But now you can't say anything longer than, "Hallelujah!"—if that. As a result, you're often more of a spectator than a participant.

How did we ever get into such a fix? Well, **around A.D. 300, the**

church made the worst blunder in her history. We *voluntarily* decided to give up the three key freedoms that powered the early church to success:
   —open worship (praising God)
   —open sharing (building up each other)
   —open ministry (serving others in the church and the world).

Throughout Christendom in the Fourth Century, we professionalized the local church and turned over our Sunday services to the pros, leaving them to do almost everything while we sat and watched.

Lay men found themselves stripped of initiative and power, like newly-captured slaves. Lay women were quietly relieved of what little responsibility and leadership they had. (By about 450, even the congregational singing faded to zip, as we turned over the music to professional choirs of men and boys.)

All the laity suddenly found Sunday worship to be more distant from their personal lives and daily concerns. They fell into Spectator Christianity, where loneliness doesn't end at church—it starts there.

The Key Malady

Today, at the end of the second millennium, we're *still* fighting the fallout from that massive mistake. Do any of these sound familiar?
   1   apathy
   2   shallowness
   3   worldliness
   4   failure to tithe
   5   pastoral burnout
   6   teenage dropouts
   7   fear of evangelism
   8   flabby self-discipline
   9   maxed-out schedules
   10 a chronic shortage of strong men.

I'm claiming that all of these maladies and more are caused mainly by one master malady: the closed church, in which laymen tend to be passive observers while ministers tend to be overworked insiders.

The Reformation was a great start on fixing the church, but it fell way short in regard to our structures.

It succeeded marvelously in getting back to sound doctrine: *sola Scriptura* (placing the Bible above the Church), *sola gratia* (salvation by grace), and *sola fide* (through faith, not works).

But it never got us back to the New Testament church pattern that we see in Paul's letters. It simply exchanged the priest for a minister and put a sermon in place of the Eucharist (Communion). And thus the reformers left behind a matched set of migraines that would give St. Paul the yips.

The good news in your hands in this book, though, is that today you can probably finish the Reformation in *your* church within a year or two—because the ten problems above don't have to be solved one by one. They're like a massive log jam that needs only one well-placed explosion to unsnarl the whole mess. By following the New Testament guidelines and opening the heart of your church to the rank and file, you can eventually:

1 Convert those mild-mannered pew warmers into spiritual warriors with clear goals and a total loyalty to your church

2 Make your services so exciting no one wants to leave

3 Help your church grow about twice as fast

4 Double or triple the number of those who tithe—and put your church finance problems in the past

5 Bring back marginal believers who quit the church long ago out of frustration or lack of interest[1]

6 Turn your teenagers into your best members (well, at least best in *some* ways!)

7 Attract more men to your church. Not J. Alfred Prufrock types, but **lions**!

8 Save your pastor from the tasks he hates and free him to concentrate on what he likes

9 Acquire a regional reputation as a rare church where one can

---

1. NEW YORK (EP)—A significant number of "unchurched" Americans feel there is not enough emphasis on spiritual experience in the churches, according to a major research project conducted by George Gallup, Jr., for 30 denominations and religious organizations.

At a news conference at the Interchurch Center, the pollster commented that "more of the unchurched than the churched have had a sudden religious experience. They're all charged up, but with no place to go."

Dr. Gallup noted that a key criticism of the unchurched in regard to religious institutions is that "churches have lost the spiritual part of religion." About one of every five unchurched persons who indicated they had "problems" with churches checked a statement which said, "I wanted deeper spiritual meaning than I found in the church or synagogue."

A summary report indicated that the...41 per cent unchurched projects to approximately 61 million [U.S.] adults. 6/24/78

find pure, uplifting worship (as in Revelation 4 and 5) along
with deep, lasting friendships

10 Enable most of your members to be soul-winners

11 End the rat race of unfocused church activities that saps the
drive of your best people

12 Create a whole new feeling of love in the congregation

This list probably strikes you as wishful thinking. I bet I know
why: because the last time a majority of our churches were successful in most of these twelve areas, Nero was burning Christians to light
his garden at night.

Actually, that's unfair. *There have been—and are now—many
churches that have made most of these changes.* Often, however, they
are overseas churches greatly purified by persecution.

In any case, the world is now careening rapidly toward a whole
new political, economic, and spiritual order, and *the fate of hundreds
of millions of souls hangs on whether or not the church is able to
gear up and capture the day.*

78 Leaking Buckets

By latest count, there are 78 plans for world evangelization created by existing churches (and parachurch organizations), each with
a budget over $100 million dollars per decade. Twenty-one of them
expect to finish the job by the year 2000.[2]

That's not to sneeze at. But to the best of my knowledge, **all of
them are designed to dump their new converts into the same old
closed-church patterns and structures that perpetuate the same
old leaky-bucket problems.** The plans themselves are quite good,
but they don't take into account the basic problem: the basis of our
operations, the church, is dynamically flawed and needs fixing. Still.
After all these centuries.

It's time to reopen our churches. This book tells you how to re-
claim your birthright—pure worship, true sharing, free ministry, and
more—<u>without</u> turning your back on the *Institutional Church,* that
nice flock of folks you sit in rows with on Sundays.

You now have a fairly rapid way to simply *erase* much of the harm
that's been done to you and others in your church. Many or most of
the quick fixes you've come across before were ways to correct your

---

2. David Barrett and James Reapsome, *Seven Hundred Plans to Evangelize the
World* (Birmingham, AL: New Hope) , $6.95.

weaknesses; what you have here is a master plan to correct the *cause* of those weaknesses.

In these pages you'll discover why the average North American church resembles the original *scriptural* church like a junked '53 Chevy resembles a Boeing 747 with a Dixieland band and 50-foot buffet. A church may have fur-lined pews, stained glass Communion cups, and a full orchestra for prayer meetings, but if it's not an *open* church, the members are being shortchanged.

PART ONE

What You've Never Been Told About Church

1
The Disastrous Success of A.D. 313: How the Church Managed to Hog-Tie Itself

A funny thing happened on the way to the Millennium: In the Fourth Century, the church's wheels fell off.

Until then, it had looked like the gospel would reach the uttermost parts at chariot race speed. Or at least before McDonald's did.

No such luck. Just after A.D. 300, the church made the biggest blunder in its history and crashed like an Indy 500 racer with a stuck throttle and a full tank of gas.

Hardly anyone knows about this blunder today except scholars (who know all about it, but discuss it just among themselves). And yet the effects were disastrous:

- Laymen lost the three key freedoms that had fueled the rapid growth: open worship, open sharing, and open ministry.
- The church degenerated from an army or family into an *audience*—overnight in some places!
- Evangelism slowed to a crawl. Or an ooze.
- Church leaders got the bright idea of diversifying into politics, and took over whole governments. We now remember this period as the, uh, *Dark Ages*.

Where Did We Go Wrong?

Within thirty years of Christ's ascension, the gospel was being preached in every outpost of the Roman Empire.

Unencumbered by mortgages, committees, staff salaries, and conflicts between choir rehearsal and church softball team practice, the "followers of the Way" blazed a trail of stunning successes.

Then as the church grew in the first three centuries, it thrived on hard times and persecution.

- In hard times, the church's strong grass-roots mutual-assistance charities held everyone together.
- In persecution, the government sharply defined the church by pushing everyone together, figuratively. And the act of taking a stand for Christ strengthened each man, woman, and child.

What was their secret? First, the presence of the living God in their hearts. Second, the weekly gathering of the church, an informal and often-boisterous affair with a full-on meal, not just a polite ceremony with an itty bitty breadcrumb and a thimbleful of Welch's. Church life was a floating party, with everyone eating dinner at each others' houses and participating 100% in the festivities.

At the weekly get-together, everyone was the star of the show, everyone was needed. Spirits were lifted, problems solved, hurts healed, hearts fed, and the Lord of lords spoke to every soul. But the *whoopee* part of the meeting, the "love-feast" (Jude 12), resembled a cross between a Super Bowl victory celebration and a frat party (with a few cups of wine instead of the keg of suds).

From our vantage point today, it looks as if they had an unbeatable thing going. A sure-fire, runaway, free-wheeling style of church that was gobbling up Satan's territory like a giant pac-man.

Why, then, did the roaring success of the early days fade? When did we cool off?

Well, as we grew larger and more popular, our feeling of being a distinct family waned. In a well-churched city, it's hard to think of everybody as a brother or sister in the Lord. "Us vs. Them" psychology doesn't work when almost everyone is us. The church became less of a revolutionary band and more of a static establishment. Eloquent preachers began to attract large followings.

The final straw came in 313, when Emperor Constantine I issued the Edict of Milan, officially tolerating the church and ending the persecutions. Church leaders from popes to local bishops got involved with the government. Many even became officials. At that time it looked like a good idea. ("Hey, we won! Now we can take over!")

As it turned out, though, it was a lousy idea. Our top leaders drifted astray on a long, long power trip and let their flocks wander.

After this first flurry of church buildings in 323-327, we ceased being an interactive family and turned into an audience. Spectators.

The Constantine Fiasco

What really killed us was the bricks.

In the biggest blunder in her history, the church began construct-
ing lots of buildings, displacing the catacombs and forest glens—and
ending forever the warm, precious, meetings in someone's living
room.

Modeled after the Roman forums, the new buildings held hundreds
of Christians. Of course, you can't have intimate, *easy* interaction
with that size crowd. So from the first Sunday it was opened, a new
sanctuary put limits on free expression. The new crib strangled the
baby. Imagine you were living in that time:

- You may have felt at ease confessing a sin to a couple dozen
  friends over at Josephus and Johanna's (or let's call them Joe
  and Jane). But in front of five hundred strangers? Whoa!
- If God taught you something this week and it lay strongly on your
  heart, you wouldn't hesitate to stand up and spend ten or fifteen
  minutes sharing it in Joe and Jane's living room. But here in the
  new hall, there are probably at least a dozen men and women with
  a message burning in their hearts. So take a number!
- Over at Joe and Jane's, everybody got into the act in the worship time. You were able to praise the Lord from your heart—
  again and again as you felt led. It was the most meaningful and
  healing moment of your week. But here? Take a number!

I could go on, but you get the idea. Without modern acoustics or
roving microphones, open meetings became difficult. Not *too* difficult, mind you, just difficult. So closed meetings took over. All
speaking became centralized in a pulpit. And order was maintained.
(Again, it seemed like a good idea at the time.)

At Joe and Jane's, you were a participant. Here, you're a spectator. A passive listener. A blip.

At first you don't mind it. The change is all so exciting. And being
with 500 believers at once—wow! Paradise! Not until years later
does it dawn on you that you've been turned into a pew potato.

But now, with 1,000 eyes focused on the pulpit, the man behind it
has become extremely important. He's very, very good, of course—
probably the best speaker in the area. His warmth and wisdom and
skill defuse any latent objections to the new state of affairs. Certainly,
his polished sermons beat the sandals off the impromptu teachings
you used to hear—and give—at Joe and Jane's.

So it doesn't take long before every local church from London to

Alexandria has its own building and its own professional Christian standing up in front every Sunday, doing most of the talking. Eventually, the love-feasts get so big and rowdy that they're banned.

No prophet or leader comes to the fore, decrying the passing of the house church or condemning the new diversion of church funds into real estate development. No one of any note questions taking initiative away from ordinary believers and bestowing it upon the new priesthood class.

And no one points out that the Holy Scriptures don't sanction any of this.

By 400, just 87 years later, the Roman Empire had gone from being less than four per cent Christian to eighty per cent Christian ... *with no conversions!* (In fact, true evangelism virtually disappeared from the face of the Earth during that time.) It was arguably the worst disaster since Noah.

Paradise Lost

All the major problems of the church today—other than sin—can be traced back 1700 years, to when the church became an audience. (Go ahead, make my day—try to think of one that can't.)

When we switched from living rooms to church buildings and professionally staffed the local church, we lost all momentum. The local church became weak and cold.

Non-priests were termed "laymen," a word not even found in the Bible—for good reason. I have struggled to find a better word to use in this book. About the best I've found is *player*, with the corresponding term for a minister being *coach*. I'll use those terms now and then. It would be nice just to call all laymen *Christians*, but what would that make your pastor? A non-Christian?

As a "layman" in a Fourth Century church building, you no longer approached God directly. The priest did so on your behalf. And thus did an architectural problem turn into a doctrinal problem. The priesthood of the believer was lost.

The Bible was taken from the hands of the layman and given to the priest. (If you're not allowed to decide what it means, why bother to read it?)

With the Scriptures out of the hands of the people, the priesthood was free to play with it unencumbered by the corrective discipline of secular life. For a thousand years, cloistered monks lovingly piled theological baggage atop the Bible until, by the time of Luther, hardly a layman in Europe knew the all-important meaning of "justification by faith."

Without the Scriptures to lift them out of the mud, laymen turned into serfs in the feudalism of the Dark Ages.

Ironically, in that darkness the only candle of hope and upward mobility was the church. Becoming a priest was the only way out of oblivion. We commonly laud the medieval church for providing this sole escape hatch from the pit; we should remember that the church helped to dig it.

The Road to Ruin

The early church had so much success and momentum that they should logically have evangelized everyone from Turkey to Tokyo by A.D. 600.

Many historians say the problem was that believers felt disillusioned when Christ didn't return right away. Well, we now have nineteen centuries of "disillusionment," and we're the biggest religion in the world.

What really went haywire? As I said, the church got so big and popular that it could erect its own buildings. Unfortunately, this solved a long-standing problem that should have been left standing: Whenever a healthy house-church got too big for its living room, it had to split—into two living rooms. *New leadership was thus always being sucked upward through the ranks.*

But when church buildings began to sprout across the Empire, congregations no longer had to face the awkward anguish of who got to stay with the favorite elders and who had to split off with the nobodies. Everybody stayed with everybody. Heavenly!

Trouble is, sharing and intimacy were tricky in a crowd of 500. And the big crowds put a premium on eloquence. So the stuttering new converts started to stay in their shells. Anonymity replaced fellowship. Communication during meetings began to be dominated by the few who could read and had access to books: In the end, that meant the priests. The laity, citizens of a long-crumbling Roman empire, were turned into spiritual eunuchs and lost the strength the empire needed so desperately at that time. By 476, Rome fell for the final time, and the church led the way into the Dark Ages.[3]

---

3. Barry Liesch points out in *People in the Presence of God* (Zondervan) that not all of the early churches had the total participation of the Greek churches

Footnote continued

The 2/3 Reformation

A thousand tear-stained years later, Luther, Calvin & Co. (bless 'em) began picking up the pieces.

They put Christian theology back together like a lovely jigsaw puzzle.

They also worked a bit on the church's practices and functions, and got about half of them glued back together, more or less. *Fabulous* work. The best fixit job since Nehemiah.

But they couldn't do everything. Rome wasn't unbuilt in a day. So the Puritans had to pick up some more pieces. In the 18th century, the Wesleys picked up some more. In the 19th century, the revivalists and missionaries picked up more. Starting in 1901, the pentecostal movement picked up even more. And the chap who founded *your* denomination undoubtedly eclipsed them all.

But there's still a gigantic hole in the church. **The "priesthood of the believer," the central goal of the Reformation, has been restored only theologically, not practically.**[4] **It still exists mainly on paper.** *In very important ways, our churches remain closed to laymen.*

Between clergy and laity there is still a big, uncrossable gap—academic, professional, and liturgical. For example:

- Even though we acknowledge the common saying, "Everyone has at least one sermon in him," almost no one is ever encouraged or even allowed to deliver that one sermon. This practice is a horrendous exercise in quenching the Spirit. It frosts me that the "one sermon" in the heart of a faithful dentist or truck driver or engineer should forever be deemed less worthwhile than all two thousand of the lifetime sermons of an M.Div.
- Most of the church is too watery to formulate and enforce *Biblical* standards for full-time ministry, so we imitate the opposition, the world. We don't allow laymen to *mature* into ministers. Jesus and Paul believed in on-the-job training; we put our faith in seminaries.

---

pioneered by Paul. The Jerusalem-oriented churches, he notes, were more like synagogues in their worship style: contemplative, not interactive.

As I see it, when large sanctuaries sprang up, the Jerusalem model quickly won the day. Sitting and listening to an eloquent orator portray the glories of God and the Christian life proved to be easier and more popular than trying to be one of 500 active participants.

4. Justification by faith was the theme. The believer's priesthood was the goal.

- We almost idolize schools and their graduates. Their lecterns are baptized as pulpits, lectures become sermons, students are parishioners, and degrees are, well, required...from *world*-approved institutions. But even in college, if you sit still for seven years, they'll give you a Ph.D. and let you stand up and do the talking. In church, you can sit for seventy years and never get to say a peep. Worse, you'll be conditioned to be *afraid* to peep. The system is *designed* to be static!
- I've even heard of churches where the rest rooms are marked for three sexes: MEN. WOMEN. CLERGY. Gimme a break!
- Odds are, God has given a handful of people in your church a gift for counseling. But odds are, that gift will never be developed to a pastoral level. The pastor will continue to be your church's counselor of first and last resort. (Question: How can he "equip the saints for the work of the ministry" when he holds a monopoly on doing so much of that work?)[5]
- You may have a retired executive who could do wonders with your church's business affairs. You'd love it if he would commit to that work. But he won't. He knows it's part of the *pastor's* job description. So the pastor will continue to get stuck with that blizzard of details until your whole church understands that *they* bear the responsibility for the work—and the pastor's only the pastor!

Free the Pastor, Free the People

Laymen today have regained the **word** of God, but not the **work** of God. The priesthood of the believer has been restored *de jure,* not *de facto.*

The very earliest Christians had plenty of problems, but the pastor-centered church wasn't one of them. Their churches were elder-led, and the burden of God's work was spread like dew on the prairie.

You can take a load off your pastor's back by changing your church into one in which the Spirit leads through your laity. You'll have a far more powerful church, one in which the workload is borne by a skilled and equipped army of laymen who know their gifts and work like troopers.

---

5. Incidentally, the one task that Scripture assigns to women is counseling younger women (Titus 2:4). But in most churches, men take even that role away from them by counseling a majority of the women themselves.

How can you do this? **Well, you can begin by opening up your worship service and granting full participation rights to all those nice folks taking up your pew space on Sunday mornings.** In other words, unlock your church and unchain the pastor. (See chapter 5, "Liberate Your Pastor!")

We didn't lose everything in the Fourth Century. Our doctrine survived well. But among the rights and privileges we lost, open worship, sharing, and ministry are the most prominent by far.

In the absence of these freedoms, your church is a closed club, and you're back to the enervating strategies we've all used in the past:

—trying just a little harder

—spending just one more hour in prayer

—witnessing to just one more person

—working just a little faster

—studying just one more chapter of the Bible per day

—wasting just a little less time

—reading one more Christian book

—serving on one more committee

... and putting more time and effort into the lives of other believers—who will then go back and rejoin the same frozen-shut system that caused the problems in the first place.

Reopening your church would be infinitely easier. Read on and see.

2
Sure, It's a Worship Service—
Says so right here in the bulletin

The early church managed the prodigious feat of being healthy without a King James Bible. Or a 700 Club. Or Fuller Seminary or Calvin's *Institutes* or Amy Grant or Winona Lake or World Vision or Sunday school buses or even one lousy church building.

The secret of their success? Every week, believers gathered for one catch-all, participatory service where they met and worshiped God heart to heart.

In that intimate communion, they gathered enormous strength directly from the Holy Spirit and shed the thousand and one cares that weigh upon the human heart. Thus transformed, they dispersed out to the community for the rest of the week as witnesses.

That was the pattern. In, out... in, out. As healthful as breathing.

In worship we turn our entire attention to God. Worship is possibly the most valuable act any human can perform, and yet today's "worship" services produce precious little actual worship in the strict sense: *praise and veneration conceived and spoken by individuals.* I've been in over two hundred traditional churches, and, sadly, found such worship in only three or four.

The great A.W. Tozer said that worship is "the missing jewel of the evangelical church." Precisely. Except for a few minutes of group singing (and perhaps group speaking in tongues), the believer normally has no chance to express his adoration and worship, to make that vital, creature-to-Creator contact. He can only listen to a leader doing these acts *on his behalf.* His worship is almost wholly vicarious.

Charismatic and pentecostal churches do allow for two or three messages in tongues, interpretations, prophecies, or "words of knowledge." These are usually given by the more advanced members, with beginners too intimidated to try. Moreover, the emphasis is on guidance (a message *from* God), not worship (a message *to* God). And of course, having such messages from fifteen or twenty people is out of the question.

You'll find pure worship in Revelation 4 and 5 and such Psalms as 23 and 139 ("O Lord, Thou hast searched me and known me...") But when these sorts of thoughts are brought into a Sunday service, they're always in music or responsive readings. Sam and Sue Christian are never allowed to choose such words and speak them from their hearts to God.

That may help to explain why the typical North American who claims to be born again can't even name the Gospels and has all the spiritual depth of a birdbath.

What to Do About It

Enable your laymen to think of themselves as actors, not spectators. You'll find more varied suggestions in Part III, but in general I would suggest three steps.

1. *You must first create a vision and thirst for involvement in worship.*

Talk with the key leaders, including the pastoral staff. Paint for them a vivid picture of what open worship could be like in your church. Together with them, make a decision to prepare the congregation for open worship, *to meet around Christ instead of having a scheduled service or program.*

Come to a general agreement on timing and strategy. Every church is different, but at some point before "opening day," you or the pastor will need to brief the congregation as a whole, and certain sensitive individuals may also need some extra orientation even before that.

Depending on the nature of your congregation, you may also want to give them some written materials on what you plan to launch, and why. In some churches, this book will be useful, perhaps ideal. In others, it would be overkill.

Your prep period could take two weeks to two months. Every church is different. But in any case, your people must *want* to grow in strength and maturity.

2. *Create a time in your Sunday worship service when the church can truly function as a body.*

Few churches will want to devote their entire Sunday service to a wide open format, especially from the start.[6] You'll need to carefully

---

6. As background information, you may be interested   *Footnote continued*

select a point or period in the service when the floor will be open.

You may want to lengthen your service. You may want to just rearrange it. Or a bit of both.

But don't make the mistake of tacking onto your calendar an extra service on Sunday evening or Tuesday morning at 6:30 "for anyone who wants to experience a new mode of worship" or whatever. They won't come. Bear in mind that the only time your church can truly function as one body is when they're all together, and that's during the Sunday a.m. meeting.

3. *Enable each person in the service to actually start making his own unique, maximum contribution to the service.*

Just telling them how will not suffice for everyone. Some things we learn only by doing. And some people learn slowly; a certain amount of behind-the-scenes coaching and hand-holding *will* be needed. Bank on it.

A majority of churches will take a few Sundays to warm up. But once they get into it, you've got a cannonball on your hands. They won't know when to stop. I was once in a large, *stand-up* prayer meeting where we simply changed the ground rules to: "Use single-sentence prayers and finish each topic before you move on." Afterward, we all thought we'd prayed 15 or 20 minutes, but it was an hour! No one could believe it.

We commonly say we're "participating" in a worship service when actually we're mostly just watching. Let's be clear on this distinction. For example, think of a pro baseball game. Do they let us spectators run out on the field and play? No way—and for good reason. I have slightly above average baseball skills, but if I were to pitch a ball to Jose Canseco, it would end up being tracked by NASA.

Participants actually affect the outcome.

---

to know that there already exists a loosely-structured denomination, called by outsiders the Plymouth Brethren, that offers unstructured worship/Communion services. In the U.S. and Canada, they have over 1200 mostly-small assemblies that meet in low-key "gospel halls" or "Bible chapels."

The PB's are arguably the most orthodox of all evangelical denominations in their worship practices. Why, then, have they not come to dominate the church scene? Among several factors, I would note that they never allow women to speak in the services, and many of their assemblies have been criticized as being not especially outgoing to outsiders.

In the face of opposition, however, the PB's have proven to be the most resilient denomination of all. They have thrived in China, where there are now possibly 30 to 50 million believers, and in the Russia, a great many of the churches officially lumped together as "Baptist" are actually PB.

Spectators don't.

Better you and I should watch in baseball, but participate in church. Yes, this can make your service a little longer. But it will add oceans of joy and excitement and spiritual growth, with deep calling unto deep. On the road to depth and maturity, you can't skip the infancy stage; before they begin to conquer principalities, they have to learn to say, "Abba, Father."

It is my firm conviction, based on experience, that nothing can be more shattering and uplifting to the human mind and spirit than a face-to-face meeting with the God of Heaven in open worship.

And true worship will plug that perpetual hole in your bucket; they'll never defect to that megachurch across town or that super-friendly little church down the road. Why? Because they will have discovered what it's like to *breathe free*, exhaling as well as inhaling.

No one else ever allowed them to do that before.

Worship, Band-Aids, and Jammed Schedules

How did the primitive church ever make it without Sunday school?... or music committees?... or high school ski conferences?... or divorce recovery workshops?

Answer: community worship met all their needs.

Today's worshipless worship meetings, however, leave a vacuum. So to compensate, we create a smorgasbord of time-gobbling activities, each of which is designed to meet a specific felt need, to make up for the absence of something a full-orbed, open service could likely do. Usually, the activity is *not* rationally planned as part of a tightly-integrated strategy to reach the world or give the devil a splitting headache or whatever.

Take Sunday school for an example. God's plan for religious education is Dad. It's a 4000-year-old plan that's worked like a watch since the days of Abraham. But if your weekly gathering doesn't equip Dad to open his mouth at home and be a teacher of the Word—well, Sunday school is your next-best bet. (Programming Dad would be easier.)

Problem is, Sunday school classes aren't your church's *raison d'etre*. Your other three dozen programs aren't either. They were launched as mechanisms to fill needs. It's a Band-Aid system.

The system does work—partly because God is very gracious and partly because we in North America produce such high quality Band-Aids.

Of course, the system does nuke your free time, tear your flock away from their unsaved neighbors (and even their own families), and imprison them behind a stained glass curtain.

In fact, as your ad hoc activities proliferate, you may find it impossible to maintain a sharp focus. You may eventually reach what Tom Sine (*The Mustard Seed Conspiracy*) calls a state of "chronic randomness," doing forty things that as a whole are less than the sum of their parts.

Solution strategy: Rather than relying on programs designed to fill holes or meet isolated needs, go for an integrated menu of high-stakes activities that directly transform hearts and pound the gates of Hell into splinters. Live dangerously, as the apostles and martyrs did.

Give up some of the predictability and safety of a rigid, fully programmed Sunday service and ask God to meet you in power as you step out in faith and learn to function as a body.

You don't need to trash your liturgy or toss your order of worship in the dumpster in order to get started. You don't need to sell the church grounds, give the proceeds to the poor, and regroup into house churches.[7] (Though you could. See chapter 12.) You don't *need* to do anything fancy.

For starters, just have a back-to-basics church with a couple of special periods in the Sunday morning schedule to allow for some open worship and open sharing. Plus a few minutes for lay ministry, like a ten-minute sermonette or a five-minute meditation as an opener for the pastor's sermon.

And make sure your elders are primed to expect miracles.

How to Create Something Eternal on Earth

It's all too easy to rob God of worship.

If we don't truly worship Him, if all our prayers drift off into petitions instead of adoration, He gets cheated. This is not a matter of tradition or preference about what we do on Sunday, it's cheating!

On the other hand, pure worship is pure gold—to Him and to us. If you've ever felt frustrated about the ephemeral nature of your earthly accomplishments, think about this: *Stand up and speak one word of worship and awe in the assembly next Sunday, and it will go down in the history of heaven as an eternal monument, a never-to-be-forgotten blessing of the everlasting Uncreated Father. Heaven won't forget, and nothing will ever erase the value of your word of praise!*

---

7. Most of those who advocate an open church favor house-churches with no staff. If Open Church Ministries has a unique position, it is that the church can regain the pluses and dynamics of the early church without abandoning its present facilities or dropping its professional staff.

3
Sharing Time:
The Exciting Fellowship
You've Always Dreamed Of

I used to attend a very good church. Friendly, growing. With a minister loved by even the worst grouch.

But though it was a model church in many ways, nothing much ever happened inside me. Their punctual "worship" services were actually a warmhearted lecture series, plus songs and offering. Almost never was I allowed to participate, except as the 387th voice in the singing.

If I'd never shown up, my absence would have been like a missing spoonful of sand from the Arabian desert. Without me, not one syllable would have changed—and that's about how significant I felt. Fact is, that's how significant I was. So I drifted away.

Likewise, **if your own church is typical, there's no opportunity for people to share their grief or joy or even the deepest needs of their short lives. They may die without anyone in church knowing the burning hopes and fears in their hearts**—simply because the pastoral staff always has the spotlight.

They don't *try* to hog the spotlight, of course. It's the closed-church *system* that forces them to center stage and consigns everyone else to the role of a mute non-person, a face without a voice or heart. It's so ironic: The *one* hour in the week when your Christian brothers and sisters all get together to interact is the *one* hour when they're prohibited from obeying the scriptural commands about interaction, like:

- Provoke one another unto good works.
- Confess your sins to one another.

- Let the word of Christ dwell in you richly as you teach and admonish one another.
- Bear one another's burdens.
- Encourage one another and build each other up.
- Respect those who work hard among you.
- Warn those who are idle ... encourage the timid.
- Pray for each other so that you may be healed.

(Not to mention, "Greet one another with a holy kiss.")

That's why today's church is dysfunctional—and has been for 1700 years. If you operate within the rules, you will find it *impossible* to obey the commands of Scripture for interaction among believers.

How can silent observers, worship service bulletin in hand, do such things?

You'd think the Holy Spirit would have made a dent in this strange system by now. But no, most Christians (including many in the ministry) seem allergic to the free-form revival that open sharing can create. I've been in a number of churches where a pastor has experimented, opening the floodgates just a crack by opening the floor to the laity for part of a meeting. It seldom fails: I see a torrent of pent-up emotions, confessions, praises, tears, new commitments, lumpy throats—and wide-eyed amazement. Instant revival!

But of course it's inherently unplanned (therefore "out of control"), so the pastor quickly reverts back to the closed format. (At least for a few months or years.) I've just never understood this.

The Impossible Situation of a Pastor

Yes, the pew can be one of the loneliest places on earth.

But sometimes the pulpit can be even lonelier. Sometimes the #1 victim of the system, the loneliest one of all, is the guy who's trying the hardest to make it all work: your long-suffering pastor.

Don't blame him! He beats his brains out in the pulpit week after week to make a difference in people's lives. But sometimes he feels like he's been condemned to a lifetime of futility, trying in vain to motivate a sullen pack of foot-dragging spiritual adolescents who never quite seem to see the big picture, never get excited enough to shoulder responsibilities, and never (by the way) come anywhere close to a 10% tithe.

Even as you read this, your pastor may be doggedly at work on Plan L (or Q or V) to light a fire under his lovable but recalcitrant flock.

His main complaint, surveys show, is that his people just don't *respond.*
I can understand that pain. When you pour out your heart, soul,
gizzard, and a wide assortment of other body parts for ten or twenty
years, and the impact and response are faint, it has to hurt—bad.

At the same time, I would point out that we're talking about an
impossible situation. When response is forbidden till the service is
over, what can you expect?

And it really is forbidden. Suppose, for instance, some gent pops
up in the middle of the sermon next Sunday and says:

Hey, great point, pastor! The Lord's been teaching me
a lot about that lately. In fact, this past week I experienced
an amazing example of what you just described. On Tuesday morning...

The nearest deacon will invite him to hit the bricks. Straightway
and forthwith. The #1 rule for laymen in closed, non-participatory
services is, "Siddown and shuddup." Yes, they're supposed to respond wholeheartedly to the sermon... but only *after* they go home
and get down to real life!

Things were different in days of yore, when the church of Jesus
Christ was turning Rome on its imperial ear. Laymen were free to
obey the promptings of the Holy Spirit and speak up when they had
something to say. They were born running—talking in church and
witnessing outside it. And in the space of three centuries, they had
conquered for Christ much of the known world, up to and including
the Emperor. Without even any *Four Laws* booklets.

That shows they were better witnesses than most Christians today.
And why? Because the church didn't stifle them. It conditioned them
to communicate their faith. Church services were different then.
Livelier. More off-the-wall. We don't have many specifics about
what they looked like, but we do have a few. Such as these...

Three Clues from Scripture

1. "When you come together, **everyone** has something to contribute: a hymn, a word of instruction, a revelation, a tongue or an interpretation... you can all prophesy in turn..."

Sunday morning in Corinth was a free-for-all, so Paul was telling
them to act more Presbyterian. But notice: He did endorse *individual
contributions by everyone.* (Do you?)

2. "While they were worshiping the Lord and fasting, the Holy
Spirit said, 'Set apart for me Barnabas and Saul...'"

This couldn't happen in the church today! Our worship patterns don't allow it, and we don't do fasts.

Our missionaries get their calls straight from God, then spend eons convincing supporters they did. If it weren't for the "extrabiblical" requirement of running around with a tin cup before getting a passport and shots, we'd have four or five times as many missionaries on the field.

3. "Speak to *one another* with psalms, hymns, and spiritual songs..." Precisely what does "one another" mean? Group singing? Hardly! Tertullian tells us what it meant in his day:

> In our Christian meetings we have plenty of songs, verses, sentences and proverbs. [*obviously individual*] After hand-washing and bringing in the lights, each Christian is asked to stand forth and sing, as best he can, a hymn to God, either of his own composing, or one from the Holy Scriptures.

Try that next Sunday!

In Tertullian's time (160-230), there were many churches that were interactive powerhouses, not audiences. So how, then, did St. Murphy's Law derail the church from such a fast track to the millennium?

Simple. By abandoning house-churches, we ran afoul of a Murphy corollary, Gall's *Non-Additivity Theorem:*

A Large System, Produced by Expanding the Dimensions of a Smaller System, Does Not Behave Like the Smaller System.

The Nuts and Bolts of Sharing

Try to envision one of your future participatory services. Here are some of the exciting components you'll see:
- individual praise and worship
- thanksgiving and testimony
- confession
- brief periods of silent meditation
- encouragement and cheer of others
- original poetry and song
- intercession
- sharing of God's lessons learned
- sharing of needs
- on-the-spot decision-making and commitments

Not all churches are ready this instant for every innovative and free mode of body life, *but all can take steps.* It's more than worth it. Just imagine. . .

- the excitement of your people praying for each other every Sunday and bearing one another's heavy loads
- the enrichment and joy of hearing what God has been teaching different families
- the thrill of seeing former fraidy-cats stand and worship the Lord, praising Him for who He is and what He's done
- the added meaning in knowing that some of the hymns and responsive readings came from the pens of believers sitting around you—or your own
- the delight of having, someday, a congregation full of impassioned and eloquent leaders (owing in part to your weekly custom of opening the pulpit to five-minute messages by members—described in the next chapter).

Sharing Kills Apathy

One problem you'll never have to worry about in an open church is apathy.

Apathy is totally impossible when you're dodging bullets. Or when you're halfway across a high wire. Or when the center snaps you the ball, and a very serious-looking 6'8" gentleman rips open the line and lunges for your throat.

The common element here is involvement. And that's the solution to apathy: total involvement. When you can stand up at your pew and look around and see scores or hundreds of people who are *committed to sharing your burden*, you've got total involvement. Ten million dollars' worth.

The vastly increased involvement that fellowship and sharing entail will sharply reduce apathy in your church—and in the long run, obliterate it.

As with your open worship time, the key will be getting a few leaders to break the ice for a few weeks. Momentum vincit omnia.

Everyone will learn that apathy is impossible when you're:

. . . standing in the congregation, praying for the father directly in front of you who has just been diagnosed as having cancer

. . . asking for prayer about getting a job to replace the one you just lost Friday

. . . speaking from the pulpit for the first time ever, giving a five-minute talk on how God saved your whole family in the past year

... volunteering to stay with a sick kid someone just told about.[8]

Like your open-*worship* period, your open-*sharing* time will add a few minutes to your schedule. Even if you want just a controlled, quasi-open time to start with, it will still stretch the service. But so what? In Russia, Christians normally meet for nearly three hours, and they pack 'em in like caviar. They must know something!

Instant Superstrength

Do you want to have the strength of ten?

Find ten people in your church who will stand *with* you, come what may. A sharing body of believers may not turn you into John the Baptist, but they will give you the ability to communicate straight from the heart without backing down from anyone or anything. And this funny phenomenon of will power is mysteriously strengthened by being a real part of a committed fellowship.

God's ideal for you and me will never be achieved through a stubborn *independence* nor a childish *dependence*. We will find maturity only in a third alternative: a healthy *interdependence*—through an incendiary fellowship in which one strong and loving heart can set fire to another.

Let's suppose we're in the same church body. That means *I'm counting on you to help me* because if we're in the same open fellowship, you're soon going to become committed to helping me. Look at what Paul says about his central message: "For what we preach is not ourselves, but Jesus Christ as Lord, with ourselves as your bondservants for Jesus' sake." (II Corinthians 4:5) I'll bet you didn't know you had a personal servant! Well, you do—me! When I accepted Jesus Christ as Lord, I also accepted my role as your servant for as long as I live. It was sort of a package deal.

Eliminate Teen Dropout

Teenagers are our most wasted resource.

They drop out of church at eighteen and don't come back until twenty-eight (with spouse and baby in tow).

At eighteen, they're 95% ready to function as adults. But no one wants to take them seriously, even in church. So they drift off. They

---

8. In a large sanctuary, fellowship usually requires roving mikes and two or three runners to tote them.

see themselves as too old for Sunday school and not old enough for church.

Solution: make sure they're integrated into your open-format time from the very first Sunday.

Prep them. Put on a three-week workshop in their Sunday school class, with hands-on training in the theory, the how-to, and the how-not-to of Spirit-led worship and sharing. Encourage the fearful. Admonish the airheads and blabbermouths. Whereas your adults need only to have a general idea of what's coming, your teens need to be well-trained and ready to contribute.

Tell them they're needed and wanted, but make sure they understand the need for restraint at their age. And show them how to blend in with what God is doing thematically on a given morning. They'll eat it up. Your adults might feel patronized, but for teens, it's rite-of-passage stuff, like keys to the car.

Make sure they understand that this is their big chance to become functional adults in one giant step. Tell them what's at stake and, like, how totally awesome the new service is going to be. (Do you know what Napoleon said was the high point of his life? His first Communion as a youth!)

If you do this right, they'll become "charter members" or "natives" of your new open church. Being young and trainable, they'll even be more valuable as participants than some older members who may drag their feet or display a persistent inability to "get with the program." They could even become your most vibrant leaders a few years from now.

You'll have to pick your adults up off the floor the first time a 16-year-old stands up and says something like:

> The stuff Mr. Wilson just said about love reminded me of John 15, where Jesus talks about laying your life down for your friends. Well, our buzz group in Sunday school was wondering last week just how anyone could really do that. I mean, you can only die for somebody once, you know. So Sherrie Turner said, "You know, our lives are made out of years and days and hours. So maybe we could lay down just a day here or fifteen minutes there." Anyway, now everybody in the buzz group is praying for some really meaningful chance every day to lay down at least fifteen minutes of our lives every day for somebody else who needs our help.

Heavy!

Once integrated, your teens will seldom drop out. Younger ones will begin to mature nicely. Older ones will slide right into their adult role—some of them even before age eighteen. (The great thing about church is, nobody checks your I.D. card.)

In fact, in three or four years, you could have the only "College & Career" group in the state filled with young adults who can stand on their hind feet and proclaim the gospel clearly, forcefully, and compassionately.

Your church won't have any more mice.

They'll all turn into lions.

4
Open Ministry: In the Steps of the Blues Brothers

Listen, and I'll tell you a shocking fact about yourself, something you never knew.

You were kidnapped as a small child, and no one ever told you about it.

You were born into a wealthy and loving family where your potential in life was awesome indeed. You lived in a huge mansion, and all the servants were anxious to help you with anything you needed. Your thoughts were welcomed, your ideas treasured, your future boundless.

With your vast resources, you could easily have become an inspiration to everyone, the sort of person poets write about. You'd have had few of the limitations you struggle with today, *and you could have helped the world immensely.*

To clarify "open ministry":

In a closed church, ministries are centrally planned by the leadership. (This does have its good points, but can fossilize quickly.) Functions are assigned. People fill slots. Thus, if a vice president of Citibank or a professor of marketing were to join a closed church, he might conceivably be greeted with, "Great! We needed a teacher for the fifth grade boys!" There's nothing wrong with helping fifth-graders, of course, but the man could likely do far more for the church.

In an open ministry church, the Holy Spirit is free to tap you on the shoulder and say, for instance, "Take a look at all those men living in cardboard boxes on South Main. I want you to start a soup kitchen for them." You're then allowed to stand during the sharing time on Sunday morning and say, "I have a burden for a soup kitchen. Does anyone else care to join me in starting one?" You're encouraged to then go before the leaders and say, "Six of us want to set up and operate a soup kitchen. Will you back us up?" The leaders then pray and seek God's face about the project. If they approve, they may commit to you the support of the congregation, moral *and* financial.

But alas, you were spirited away to live with a poor and eccentric family of kid-swipers who took a liking to you. They lived at the end of a dead end road in a big old house that never knew an architect, just a series of single-minded occupants who tacked on whatever additions they needed at the time.

They were a large and friendly family that took decent care of you, but in a stifling sort of way. The most exciting thing that ever happened to you was watching the tar come up through the cracks in the street on a hot day. They meant well, but the main rule in the house was, "Behave yourself and be quiet!" Worst of all, they've kept you in the dark about your real identity to this day.

It's hard to be mad at folks you love—especially those who adopted and raised you, but then it's hard *not* to be mad when you think of what's happened to you:

- Your self-image has been miniaturized.
- You've been cut off from your brothers and sisters.
- Your potential has been shrunk dramatically.
- Your role in history may be headed for the wastebasket.
- You've lost your past, your future, and your birthright.
- A lot of your time and money was wasted.
- And they've convinced you that all this was done for your own good!

It's hard not to be angry.

Now, the reason you don't remember any of this is that it occurred right after you were born ... but of course I'm talking about your new birth, your spiritual birth into the great and magnificent family of God, where freedom is the rule and only Jesus Christ is Lord.

As a member of that family, you had all the rights and privileges of royalty, such as:

- *Servants!*—millions of brothers and sisters worldwide, dedicated to loving and serving you day and night.
- *High Standing*—instant respect and a listening ear from everyone. No one but the Lord Himself outranked *you!*
- *Personal Impact*—powerful involvement in others' lives. Heart to heart, life-changing sharing with many people.

And the nice family of shleps that kidnaped you—well, I'm afraid that was the Institutional Church, a warm-hearted but professionally-run organization that froze into a closed form by the end of the Fourth Century.

At their gatherings, you had the right to remain silent, and not a whole lot more. Your royalty was never recognized. You were treated amiably, but like a commoner. Well, actually, the term they used was *layman*.

Only one problem with that: You're **not** a layman or laywoman. You're **royalty**, a child of the King, and don't you ever forget it! The whole concept behind the word "layman" is spurious and harmful, and I'd like nothing more than to erase it from memory.

Why do I want to wipe out all Christian laity? Four reasons. The category of "layman" (and laywoman) is:

1. **Unscriptural.** The Greek root word for laity is "laos," and it simply means "people." It has nothing to do with not being in the ministry.

2. **Dead wrong.** If you're an earnest Christian, you *have* a ministry (I Corinthians 12:7,11,13,27).

3. **Negative.** It defines you by what you *aren't*.

4. **Offensive.** The connotations of *layman* are in the same ballpark as *peon, peasant, amateur, yokel,* and *the great unwashed.*

Sorry to be so wordy here, but this is a major point. You must realize that *although you may not make your living from the church, you are a minister of the gospel.*

A ministry is simply the sphere in which you exercise your gifts. And you *do* have a spiritual gift. You do! You do! You do!

The Church with No Laymen

In a big old house on embassy row in Washington, D.C., you'll find the Church of the Saviour, a small Presbyterian church that has been written up in many magazines and several books.[9]

They wouldn't claim to be perfect, but they sure do a lot of things right. So far, they've split off eight new congregations in order to remain small. And aspiring members must wait up to two years before acceptance—including 55 weeks of classes! Before Constantine, converts often had quite a wait before they could join a church, but in this era, Church of the Saviour stands out like a plaid pig.

Their secret of success is that nobody can join without also joining one of their mission groups (of about four to eight people). Even the minister, Gordon Cosby, belongs to one.

Each group has a double focus. First, it has a task. Groups form when someone feels led to undertake a mission (like starting a coun-

---

9. The best two are by Elizabeth O'Connor: *Call to Commitment* ($7.95) and her later *Journey Inward, Journey Outward* ($8.95), both from Harper & Row.

seling hotline) or shoulder a responsibility (like maintaining the church facility). He or she issues a call for other members to join in the new task; if enough respond, the group begins. That's the outward focus.

Second, the group meets once a week to compare notes. Everyone keeps a spiritual journal. They share their personal progress and problems, and support each other. That's the inward focus.

Laminating the inward and outward is very, very smart. It enables them to avoid extremes: the hollowness of a works-oriented group and the self-centered introspection of a talk group.

Now, any healthy church will eventually help its members find a ministry and achieve inner growth. But Church of the Saviour, by *requiring* you to find a fellowship-ministry upon joining, has got it down to a fine art. If a layman is someone not in ministry, then it's fair to say they have no laymen.

(By the way, what does your church *require* of its members? Anything at all? Or is it content to have many who are just spectators? Think about it.)[10]

Ministry Starts at the Heart of the Church

With wide variations, your adventure toward creating an open church may include three steps or phases:

1. Preparing for—and launching—a period of open worship in your regular Sunday service.

2. Preparing for—and launching—a second period, devoted to "body life" fellowship. (This requires that your people begin to "bear one another's burdens." If they aren't ready to start doing that, you can put your "body life" plans on the shelf until they are.)

You may designate just one period as worship and body life combined, but you'll still find that your people will tend to start with one and end with the other.

3. During all the growth and excitement, many people will rapidly develop their long-repressed spiritual gifts. They will start doing so in

---

10. A church that requires heavy commitments (e.g., 20% of income, 10 hours a week distributing tracts, 100% meeting attendance) is being run like a cult. On the other hand, the typical evangelical church, with no ongoing requirements at all, tends to have the same mutual love and commitment as the rush hour gang on the freeway. My personal opinion is that we're never going to be strong enough to win the Muslim and humanist world until we find a middle road—like Church of the Saviour—with modest but firm requirements.

Why are we so afraid of commitment? I just saw a license plate frame in my church parking lot that echoes the problem: "Smile! It's not a commitment."

the very first hour of your new worship services. In short order, however, they will also start exercising those gifts outside the service:
- preparing questions for their first home Bible study group
- painting a house for a shut-in
- recruiting an outreach team
- visiting those in prisons, as Christ expects
- counseling a suicidal teenager on the church's hotline
- handing out tracts
- organizing a letter writing campaign to combat a social evil

...and much more—especially if you're sharp enough to encourage them. Although the worship service is an end in itself, it should lead to other avenues of service, or something's haywire.

If you're a typical pastor, you're often frustrated by your people's lack of eagerness to get into such activities. What you may not be taking into account fully is that *deep involvement has to start at zero hour (11 a.m. Sunday) at Square One (in the sanctuary) with a real-life, acted-out, spoken, functional acceptance into the innermost heart of the congregation.*

In fewer words, **we absolutely must let each believer take full part in the heart of congregational life by speaking words of his own.** (Try to imagine a home where only the father could talk, and the mother and kids could only chant in unison.) If we do this much, the Holy Spirit will take it from there.

One suggestion: If you're really afraid you'd have some over-long contributions, you might adapt for your use what Pastor Jack Hayford did at The Church on the Way, in Van Nuys, California, to handle *revelations from God*, a specialty in pentecostal and charismatic churches. He asked people to quietly share their message with an elder in the service *before* they spoke up—to make sure it seemed authentic. At first they were fearful this requirement would make people clam up, but to everyone's surprise, it actually freed people to speak up more often because the elders' enthusiastic approval released them from the fear of saying something stupid! You could have a similar requirement for *any* contribution longer than, say, three or four minutes. I don't think this is necessary for most churches, but it may allay leaders' fears.

A Few Practical Steps

Open your pulpit. In addition to launching open worship and body life segments in your Sunday service, take two more steps:

1. Each week, feature one or two 5-minute messages from your laymen. "Sermonettes" or whatever.

2. And when your laymen become skilled enough, have a "laymen's Sunday" every two or three months, featuring full sermons by laymen.

Unless your church positively forbids it, include your laywomen. But in all churches, men should be especially encouraged to exercise their natural role as leaders. Even staunch Christian feminists are glad to see men being men—as long as women are not held back.

Get with the program. Allow a few of your reader types (men and women) to form a "Global Intelligence Team." See Appendix B.

Share the official-looking activities. In I Corinthians 14, it's obvious that when "the whole church comes together" (v.23) *anybody* could chip in with a psalm, a revelation, or just about anything else. But the Corinthians didn't have much in the way of ritual, so that wasn't mentioned. Today, we have ceremonies and officialized customs, so perhaps we need to kind of write them into I Corinthians 14:26. George Larsen, a reader from California, wrote me his view on this sort of practice:

> What takes place at the Lord's Table is the ultimate act of spiritual worship, and any attempt to take over and run things with certain select persons in charge makes it <u>your</u> table. The one who is moved by the Spirit to give thanks for the loaf is the appropriate one, and he addresses the Lord Jesus Christ in recognition of His presence in our midst—Matt. 18:20; Luke 24; John 20:19. He then breaks the loaf and passes it to the assembly...

Certainly not every denomination will be comfortable with this degree of freedom, but if yours is, plow ahead! Life will never look the same to you again.

Paint the big picture. Let your congregation know the lid is off. Give them an array of ministry ideas (like those from the Global Intelligence Team). And give them some mechanism to launch these ideas, like the practice at the Church of the Saviour, where someone stands up and issues a call for others to join him in a task. *Aim at some kind of ministry for everyone, not overcommitment and burnout for the few activists.*

Don't be bashful about privately suggesting a ministry to someone if you think he or she would be just right for it.

And finally, never become so excited about what God is doing in your midst that you neglect outreach and compassion ministries. A heart for the suffering world is an unfailingly healthy sign.

Branch out. Divide and conquer. Encourage your men to become leaders by spearheading new satellite congregations. That's clearly a Biblical pattern.

As they create these new fellowships, have them bear in mind the example of Alcoholics Anonymous. AA avoids many a problem by owning no buildings, keeping no membership data, and hiring no professionals. Laymen run the entire movement and devote almost all their time to their message and mission.

Teamwork. Inevitably, God will bring you a few challenges that transcend any small group and require the whole congregation to work together. Let's focus on one big area, personal evangelism—and the fear thereof. Allow me to go far afield for a good example:

From 1961 to 1979, M.Y. Chan worked in a night soil pit in China.

That means he spent six to eight hours a day standing in human excrement with no protection, filling buckets with waste to be spread on fields as fertilizer. Not a fun gig.

His huge prison camp in Kiangsu province had four main latrine areas, and they all drained into one horrendous hellhole where he stood every day in sludge sometimes up to his waist.

Chan was singled out for this punishment as a Chinese pastor with a church of 300. But because his church knew of his plight and stood with him, he survived those 18½ years without one sick day! Moreover, his parishioners witnessed like tigers and grew to 5,000 in his absence!

Now 58, he has churches in twenty locations, each with about a thousand believers.

From a human standpoint, the three "keys to success" were:

1. His church knew about his troubles.
2. They supported him in prayer.
3. Because of that unity, they became extremely bold in witness.

If your pastor were sent to prison for his Christian stand, would it have the same galvanizing effect on *your* people? Of course, you don't want him to go to prison. But you do want your people to see themselves as an integral part of the exciting things God is doing in the dark, faraway places. It will revolutionize them.

A solution to the witnessing willies: Move your troops' hearts to the front lines where they can stand with the bravest of the brave. Teach them to support the heroes in God's "War for the World" by fighting alongside them. Help them show solidarity with your brothers and sisters in tough places around the globe.

Finding a steady supply of heroes will be a good ongoing project for your Global Intelligence Team, by the way. They'll discover there have been 325,800 Christians martyred per average recent year.[11] (On the bright side, they'll find, for example, that there are about 23,000 new Christians in mainland China <u>every day</u>—a growth rate about six times higher than the country itself!)

Hero stories abound. In time, your congregation will find it easier to witness boldly because they'll see themselves as part of a winning global mission of brothers and sisters, not as lone oddballs.

How to Be 20,000% Stronger

Their witnessing will also be strengthened by the fact that they're getting regular Sunday practice in proclaiming the whole counsel of God.

As they get better and better, this will take a lot of pressure off the pastor's sermon performance. <u>Although we greatly need preaching of the Word, that's no reason to have worship services totally dominated by virtuoso sermons.</u>

In the dark and middle ages, the only guy in church worth listening to was the only one who could read. But today in North America we have nearly full literacy and a crying need to widen our "resource base." That means lay participation. In a church of 200, for example, you can multiply your resources 20,000% simply by not holding people back any longer!

What happens when a man sits in a pew for fifty years? He gets thoroughly programmed, *but only on his input circuit.* He opens his mouth to witness, and—wonder of wonders—nothing comes out. He scratches his head and says, "Darn! I *know* all that stuff."

However, after a few months of participation, thinking on his feet, he will have some practice using his output circuit, and evangelism will come more easily. And if he has a *gift* for evangelism, his entire life will take on new meaning. He will bloom like a hillside of edelweiss.

In the Steps of the Blues Brothers

Remember Jake and Elwood?

A few years ago there was this hilarious comedy about two brothers who were non-violent criminal types. In most repects, they were

---

11. From a conversation with David Barrett, the leading authority in that area.

totally out of touch with the normal world of morals, so much so that they were classic corrupt buffoons.

But early in the film, they pay a visit to their one remaining contact with conventional morality, a surrealistically tough and abrasive nun who had been their parochial school teacher. She browbeats them (literally, with a ruler) into undertaking a campaign to raise funds for the school. The rest of the movie is escapades and misadventures, as they obediently cut a swath of chaos in their amoral fund-raising efforts, leaving behind crowds of irate music fans, frustrated SWAT teams, and the biggest pile of wrecked police cruisers ever created in Hollywood.

Two more unlikely characters could not have been found to portray Christian fund-raisers than the stars, Dan Akroyd and the late John Belushi. These two bequeathed to Western culture one memorable running gag line. Whenever they met someone who needed an explanation of their incredible activities, they off-handedly replied, with quiet sincerity, "We're on a mission from God."

What made the line so funny was its total absurdity, coming from two bozos who were oblivious to anything remotely spiritual. To any normal viewer (if normal people watch Belushi movies), being on a mission from God is such an exalted idea that it doesn't belong in the same universe with losers like Jake and Elwood.

In fact, being on a mission from God sounds so sacred to most of us that it doesn't even belong on the lips of average *churchgoers*. And that's the problem here. It may be hard for you to fully accept, as you begin to minister to others with your God-given gifts and abilities, that you really *are* being sent by God Himself. After all, how often have you ever undertaken an effort where you could look people in the eye and explain, with a straight face, "I'm on a mission from God"?

Yet that is what you must realize now. If you don't, then you will look upon every ministry task as just one more pet project of your own devise. (And if it doesn't succeed, so what?) When you meet with difficulties, you will face them as a commoner, a layman, an amateur, a pretender who is way out of his league, like the Blues Brothers. And you may very well fold.

That won't do. Without getting a swelled head, you must remember that you are *royalty;* you are doing precisely what you were created for, and, somehow, it is all very important to the Lord of Hosts, who gave you all your abilities and who never makes mistakes.

5
Liberate Your Pastor!

Your Pastor Jones is there at each bedside in illness and death. He's there as a wise counselor at crucial turning points. He's there to point inquirers to the cross after evangelistic sermons.

Good old Pastor Jones—he's there for everything!

Unfortunately, that means a lot of your church's spiritual experience is funneled through him. Thus he keeps growing faster than your laymen. Thus the clergy-laity gap is self-widening.

Laymen in your church usually ease the pain of that gap by identifying with the pastor. It's less frustrating for them if they just learn to experience much of the Christian life through him; after all, they can't do everything the pastor does, so why try?

Paul Tournier once put his finger on this maddening problem. This is worth reading twice:

> Even the most saintly and humble person—the revered and much loved leader of a devoted congregation—inevitably makes his followers dependent upon him, like little children. It is not his faults, but his virtues, his fame and his richness of spirit, which hold them back and prevent them from growing up themselves. They will do so only when he is gone.

Translation: The greater the pastor, the more dependent the laymen! The greater he becomes, the wider the gap. Sad but true. Unless he is that rare exception who can transmute followers into leaders, his followers will remain hunched in his shadow—because they like it there.

Your Alter Ego in the Pulpit

The pastor serves a vicarious function like a second self, a designated saint, a spiritual proxy.

By his exemplary and important life, he "lifts" the whole congregation. Each person feels the pastor is "a part of me" somehow—a vibrant, solid, undefiled, strong part of me.

Every pastor knows the admiration and adulation that goes with the job. (It helps compensate for the long hours, heavy demands, and never-quite-enough salary.) Watching him in the pulpit is emotionally like going to a play and identifying with the main character.

I am not decrying this psychological processs. It's healthy. It's needed. But it must be spread around. If all the admiration in your church is always focused on your pastor, you've got a sick state of affairs.

To be specific, if Mike and Mary Lunchbucket can sit in your church for sixty years and never have anyone come up to them and say, "I really appreciated what you said in church today," you're creating spiritual midgets. You're starving them to death in the pews. You're stomping on their hands as they grasp for a tiny shred of their share in the spiritual life of the congregation.

Am I being overly dramatic? Sure. But if you're Mike or Mary and you're eighty years old and facing the end of your life and you've just come to realize you've only achieved a tiny fraction of your potential and you're sitting here reading about open churches for the first time in your life, you can probably think of some comments that are even more dramatic than mine.

The Medium Is the Mess

When the pastor stands in the pulpit to preach, his mind is filled with all the right things: the person of Christ, salvation, the cross, eternal life, freedom from sin, a new life of joy, etc.

But that's just speech, one avenue of communication. There's also the body language, seating arrangements, social impressions, clothing, group actions, expectations of response, time limits, symbolic actions, emotional ties, and other dimly-understood semantic processes going on.

So the message may be fine, but all this other stuff can almost overwhelm it. The facts of the message tend to get obscured by the overpowering wattage of the churchy medium, namely that you're sitting there in rows in fancy clothes, doing nothing but listening to a gentleman who is doing nothing but standing behind a wooden box and talking. In other words, the medium is the message, and the #1 *nonverbal* message is that you have nothing worthwhile to say—

which is in direct conflict with the message that Christ has redeemed us to be His fully-functioning body.

The Pastor As Hub

Let's shift from the psychological level to the organizational.

In any fair-sized, pastor-centered church, you'll find an elaborate program revolving around one highly-trained, overworked man or woman.

Typically, he dominates the Sunday meeting. The usual result: The laity suffers, in the words of C.S. Lewis, from "shriveled manhood."

But the pastor suffers, too. He's only one person, and when you make him ultimately responsible for all your programs and goals, you overload an extremely valuable servant of the Lord and diffuse his talents into a sieve. The reason he went to seminary was to learn to *guide* a spiritual steam roller, not *push* it. (And definitely not carry it!)

Too many capable pastors have been fired because they came to be seen as the fall guy for the predictable failure of a jumble of clashing programs. Thousands of competent ministers have seen their careers crash because they were blamed for the chronic inertia of a flock of wing-clipped birds forbidden to fly.

That should never happen. And in fact, in an open church it's highly unlikely—because progress is viewed as *everyone's* responsibility, from the least to the greatest.

"Whoever would be great among you must be your servant." A servant is a minister and vice versa. A true minister leads by example and by coaching/equipping/teaching others in the right direction.[12]

In a scriptural style church, he doesn't lead by hierarchical authority because he doesn't have much of it. The hierarchical authority lies—*if anywhere*—with the elders. If it didn't, Paul would have directed Titus to go all over Crete and appoint *pastors* in every town, not elders. (Titus 1:5)[13]

---

12. The prolific Lawrence O. Richards has written (with Clyde Hoeldtke) *the* book on true Christian leadership: *Church Leadership* (Zondervan, 400 pp., $16.95). Out of the 118 books he's written, this is close to the best. Guaranteed to clear up your sinuses.

13. Actually, *elder, bishop, overseer,* and *pastor* are interchangeable if not synonymous in Scripture, as many commentators have noted. If you compare Titus 1:5-9, Acts 20:17, 28-30, and I Peter 5:1-3, you'll see how these terms slosh around and overlap. Peter (Catholicism's first Pope) even placed himself on the same level

Footnote continued

And if we're supposed to center our church operations around our pastors, how come the word "pastor" only shows up once in the New Testament—in passing—as part of a list of gifts? I keep hoping that someday some famous theologian will note that the Bible has a whole string of requirements for elders, bishops, and even deacons—but none at all for pastors...and draw the logical conclusion.

Equipper, Enabler, Example—But Not a C.E.O.

Don't expect your pastor to wave a magic wand and make all this happen for you. He's only one guy, and you can't expect him to do everything.

I am not saying you should attempt to work around your pastor, much less gang up on him, but just don't expect him to spearhead any revolutions for you. In fact, if he's new to his post or doesn't resonate with the idea of the open church, he may even be feeling insecure about the long term prospects for keeping his job. I firmly believe that in the truly open church, a well-ensconced pastor need not fear for his job because there is such a bottomless need for proactive counseling, "equipping the saints for the work of the ministry."

Right now, in all likelihood, your minister is extremely busy, and his individual counseling is limited to reactive type cases, putting out fires, handling crises, and keeping lives and homes from falling apart. He would *love* to be able to transpose into the kind of powerful *personal* ministry that he used to dream about in seminary, and the open church is the only kind that will usually enable a senior minister to do that.

The open church would allow him, for just one example, to call in all the men in the church[14] for individual *spiritual* counseling. He could:

    1. find out, often for the first time, where each one is spiritually

---

as an ordinary elder: "To the elders among you, I appeal as a fellow elder... Be shepherds of God's flock that is under your care, serving as overseers ... not lording it over those entrusted to you, but being examples..." (*NIV*)

So how did we ever fall into a pattern of hierarchical rulers wearing funny hats? The answer is quite fuzzy, but historian F.F. Bruce points to St. Ignatius, who early in the Second Century appointed bishops with the responsibility of combating heresies, saying: "If in each church no one was allowed to administer baptism or the eucharist, or even preside at an *agape*, except the bishop... undesirable doctrines would be effectively excluded."

14. As noted elsewhere, Scripture gives older women the job of counseling women.

2. enable him to bury his past (healing of memory, etc.)
3. find out where he wants to go
4. help him pull up the weeds in his life, and
5. equip him to move toward his goals.

Most of the men in a typical church have never had five minutes
of in-depth pastoral counseling. So as you can imagine, these five
steps alone could revolutionize the whole assembly—and give the
men plenty to share about in the open meetings!

A Modest Proposal

Want to do your faithful pastor a little favor? Fire him.

Then hire him back—as your minister. Or chief equipper (Eph.
4:12). Or enabler specialist. Or consultant in spiritual husbandry.
Or liaison between heaven and earth. Or *anything* that emphasizes
his spiritual ministry!

Actually, I suppose "pastor" is a nice, warm title. But do absolve
him of the responsibility for all the administrative and procedural flot-
sam floating around your church. Relieve him of the sole responsibility for the success of everything in sight: the men's golf fellowship,
the new building fund, the choir retreat, hospital visitation, vacation
Bible school, the stewardship committee, the works.

Tell him you only expect one thing of him: to turn everybody into
a spiritual giant. Or at least a spiritual Hulk Hogan.

Then get busy and make that possible. Take some of the steps you
read about in previous chapters. Tell the congregation to put on their
boots and crampons, grab an ice ax, and get ready to climb a very
tall mountain. Quote for them Hebrews 10:38, "But My righteous
one shall live by faith, and if he shrinks back, My soul has no pleasure in him."

Oh, and give your minister a little raise. I guarantee you'll be
getting more results for your money.

PART TWO

From Participants to Spectators: The Incredible Untold Story of How We Got So Far Off the Track

Welcome to Part Two, the most shocking section of the book.

By now, I hope you've found that it's not designed to pile yet another layer of goosefeathers on top of the institutional church, but to peel away the gummy shell of traditions which have encrusted the *real* church to the place where you need a team of archeologists (literally) to find the original shape.

You're about to find out how artificial that shell really is.

Just remember, this isn't criticism, it's plain history, history as you've probably never seen it before.

Grab your smelling salts and dive in!

6

The Emperor's New Church: The Naked Truth about How Constantine Stripped the Church of Its Power and Reclothed It with Invisible Finery

by Gene Edwards
with humor and comments by James Rutz

Most of what you do today as a participant in the church was set in concrete during two short periods of history, neither of them in the New Testament period.

The first was A.D. 323-327, and it was almost all bad. Dreadful, actually.

The second was the fifty years following October 31, 1517, and it was a mix of bad and good.

This chapter is about the first, the next chapter is about the second.

Constantine became Caesar of the Roman Empire in 306 , the biggest turning point in church history—a downward turn, by the way.

And on October 31, 1517, a date symbolically denoting the beginning of the Reformation, Luther nailed ninety-five subjects he would like to debate (all written in Latin) onto a church door.

Those two periods of time are like two gigantic cauldrons out of which have flowed most of the practices of present-day Christianity (not its theology, mind you, but its practice).

A few of our present practices were introduced in the Middle Ages (like the education of the clergy). And a few things evolved in the last hundred years or so, some even in the last forty years. But in the greater scheme of things, these two periods formed most of what you see when you watch the church in action today.

Let's look first at the pre-Constantine age, 100-313, and then at the age of Constantine, including the years immediately thereafter.

Once upon a time, Christians used to do lunch with lions.

And we were the lunch.

Such heavy persecution was unusual, though, despite what Hollywood says. In fact, it was quite sporadic for most of the first three centuries. And even in the worst times, there were many areas where the authorities simply didn't bear down on us at all.

But then came February 23, 303. Now *that* was persecution. On that date, Diocletian, who was otherwise a pretty good emperor, signed his first general edict against Christians.

This edict mandated that all copies of the Scriptures were to be burned, that all Christian worship be banned, all meeting places closed, and all church leaders rounded up wholesale and forced to recant. The torture and bloodshed were so great that even the pagan citizens were sickened and repulsed.

The worst part of Diocletian's persecution was that it crippled our leadership and left the church with her guard down, wide open to the tragedy that quickly befell her when Constantine, professing to be the first Christian emperor, came along and befriended the beleaguered leaders. He took over as undisputed emperor after his victorious battle at the Milvian Bridge in 312. At that time, apparently, not a single prophet was left to arise and denounce what took place under the new regime.

Constantine has been called the first "medieval" believer. That means, roughly: complete dedication, little knowledge, less fruit. He had the mind of a Caesar (an emperor). He had absolute authority in everything, and that definitely included the empire's Department of Religion.

Secondly, he also had the mind of a pagan, which sees a world filled with darkness, spookiness, weirdness, ghosts, apparitions, worship of idols and magic—in a word, superstition. In another word, paganism! Yes, he was reported to have had a sudden and miraculous conversion upon beholding a cross appearing in the heavens that bore the inscription, "By this sign shalt thou conquer (*in hoc signo vinces*)." But this tradition is very doubtful, and the fact is that he had very little Christian understanding to enlighten his pagan values.[15]

He was also a megalomaniac. For example, in one of his grander church buildings, he set thirteen statues of the "thirteen apostles," he himself being the thirteenth and having a larger statue than all the others!

Blend all that together, and you have the basic ingredients of medieval "Christianity," a blight that eventually spread across Europe on a grand scale. It was a mixture of Christian faith, paganism, and the values of the Roman Empire, which all flowed together to produce the Christian worldview of post-A.D. 500. (That outlook did begin to change again, arguably, not long before Luther nailed those ninety-five theses on the door of the Wittenberg church.)

The Years When the Church Collapsed

Let's look now at this watershed period in church history. We picked up more traditions, made more blunders, and changed the course of the church more radically from 323 to 327 than in any other period of history. Look what happened during this time.

- Constantinople was founded in 323.
- The first church buildings ever erected on this planet were planned and begun in 323.[16]
- The first Council of Nicaea occurred in 325.
- In 326 Constantine's mother made a trip to the Holy Land (becoming the first Christian tourist), to seek out the place of Christ's birth and crucifixion.

---

15. *Tedious footnote for historians:* These two chapters aren't intended to be a balanced dissertation showing the evidence for and against everything. History books do that very well, but this is just a short, popular summary of the evidence about man-made customs in the church, trying to show events as clearly and forcefully as possible. It's possible, for example, to give much evidence to suggest Constantine was a brave and sincere Christian. Unfortunately, the preponderance of evidence shows that his motivations were mixed—mixed with large doses of paganism. Also, any reading of church history will show that God has been infinitely powerful and gracious in working through the church, His bride, during even the worst periods and through the most flawed structures. And the very institutions skewered in these pages (sermons, choirs, etc.) have been used by Him to draw millions of people to Himself. Praise to His name for each one!

If you feel a strong loyalty to the customs discussed in these two chapters, you may be bothered by the zest with which they are dispatched. But when you examine the evidence closely, you must conclude that, on balance, it is inescapably negative. —J.R.

16. See in bibliography, Graydon F. Snyder, *Church Life Before Constantine.*

● Finally, in 327 Constantine left Rome and bequeathed his palace to Sylvester, the senior minister of the church in Rome.

When Constantine founded the city of Constantinople (Istanbul), he planned a gigantic capital which he called New Rome. It sat, literally, half in the Orient and half in the Occident.

He built a new and uninhabited city from the ground up. In it he commissioned the building of pagan temples and something he designated as buildings for Christians to meet in.

A pagan temple of that time was a small, round building with stairs leading up to an altar in the middle. Usually the people gathered around the temple and worshiped while standing outside. Across the street from some of these pagan temples, Constantine commissioned Christian meeting places. These were not shaped like pagan temples, but like the government civic auditoriums. (Christians had met inside for three centuries. But it was inside **homes**.) Here, for the first time, stood officially designated places for Christians to meet. This was a wonder which no Christian had ever seen before. Put another way, *it was in 323, almost three hundred years after the birth of the church, that Christians first met in something we now call a "church building." For all three hundred years before that, the church met in living rooms!*

Constantine built these assembly buildings for Christians not only in Constantinople, but also in Rome, Jerusalem, and in many parts of Italy, all between 323 and 327! This then triggered a massive "church building" fad in large cities all over the Empire. Many thousands of pagans came into these buildings. One could only wish they had all become saved and grown to maturity.

In his pagan mentality, Constantine ordered each building to be named after one of the Christians in the New Testament. Why? Well, mark the answer well: because pagan temples had always been named after pagan gods. So the builders put a word like "Joseph" on the front of each building, or "Mary" or "Peter" or "Paul," just as pagan temples had on them "Apollo" or "Zeus." The die was beginning to be cast. We were headed straight for a totally different kind of Christian worship in a wholly different atmosphere from what the first century believer had ever dreamed of.

Incidentally, researchers have recently discovered that only *after* Constantine slapped Biblical names on his Constantinople church buildings did gentile Christians begin to name their children after Biblical characters. Until that time, believers had always given local or family names to their children. After Constantine, Christians fell into pagan ways of naming. (Pagans had long named their children after religious figures, and we simply began to copy them.)

Constantinople was finally completed, and people moved there in droves from Rome. Imagine a typical Christian walking into one of these strange looking "Christian buildings." He had never seen anything like this! I suppose he walked into the building and sat down on the cold stone floor. (Constantine had forgotten to invent the pew.) This definitely was no comfortable living room.

In fact, trying to figure out whether to sit on the cold floor or stand throughout the whole meeting (as the pagans did across the street) caused one of the great debates and marked differences between the Eastern church and the Western church. The Italians dragged in benches and got comfortable. The Greeks stood up. (The Western church grew, the Eastern church didn't!)

By now people were coming into the church *en masse* out of paganism, following the strong example of their emperor, Constantine. The church was changing to accommodate them, introducing structure and ritual into the meetings, with chanting and pageantry—all things familiar to these ex-pagans. The *clergy*—this very word had previously been used to designate a pagan priest—began to wear strange clothing (costumes, if you please) to set themselves apart from the laity. Church buildings sprouted up everywhere on the crest of state tax money pouring into the church's coffers all over the Roman Empire. Soon the living room church meetings were but a memory, and even that memory seems to have been stamped out.

Until that time, any tax money that went to religion had been channeled exclusively to the pagan religions. By A.D. 400 it flowed exclusively to the church. Pagan priests were suddenly becoming "Christians" to keep up with the whereabouts of their money. Government officials and politicians were becoming Christian priests in droves because it was lucrative to do so.

A.D. 380 is the date when you could probably say that Christianity became the state religion of the Roman Empire. Or you might put it another way: In 380, Christianity was merged with the pagan Roman state religion.

Now, if you are *exceptionally* quick, you may be asking yourself, "And just when was Christianity unmerged from paganism? When did the Church repudiate and divorce herself from neo-paganism?" Well, I'm still researching that one. If I ever come across an unmerge date, I'll be sure to let you know.

By the mid-400s, the pagan temple's choir was also transplanted over into the Christian buildings.

So was the *ambo*. What's an ambo? You know it by the name *pulpit*.

Always on Sunday

To emphasize the homogenous nature of the new pagan-Christian religion, the state decreed that the first day of the week would be a holiday.

The idea was to encourage pagans to observe it along with Christians. Rather than calling it "the Lord's Day" or something, they retained one of the names that had been used for a couple of centuries, *dies solis*, the "day of the Sun." Pagans were used to worshipping the Sun, not Jehovah, so the state gave preference to them on this point.

Thus to this day, we pay unwilling homage to the Sun on Sunday, along with the Moon on Monday, plus a mini-pantheon of Norse, Teutonic, Germanic, and Roman gods: Tiu, Woden, Thor, Frigg, and Saturn.

Sleep well tonight. In case there's anything to these other religions, we're covered.

Where Did Our "Order of Worship" Come From?

Around A.D. 500, a gentleman whom history has given the name Gregory the Great was serving as bishop of Rome.

At that time Rome had long lain in ruins and wasn't much more than a cow pasture. Yet despite this, the power of the bishop of Rome was growing. Gregory invented an order of worship and then decreed that it would be the *only* one for all churches in Christendom.

For Catholics, that "order of worship" has not been changed in fifteen hundred years. But dead or alive, it is repeated every Sunday in literally millions of places.

But before you (likely a Protestant) say "tut-tut" at such lifeless ritualism, you should know that Martin Luther and John Calvin invented the Protestant way of worship, and it hasn't changed in over four hundred years! Furthermore, it is just as unimaginative, ossified, hidebound, ridiculous, boring, dead, and irrelevant to modern man as what Gregory invented!

It's a funny thing about religion: Once "deified," certain elements never change. A total revolution is needed in the way Christians gather. But rejoice! An exciting new Christian revival—the open church life—now brings with it an *infinite* number of ways to gather and to worship.

Where We Got the Sermon

Let us look at one last man of this era. He and his contribution are often overlooked. I refer to John Chrysostom, who bequeathed to us *Christian oratory*.

Unlike the other traditions I mentioned so far, this one might appear at first glance to be very scriptural. The powerful sermons of Spurgeon, Ironside, and Jonathan Edwards, for example, will reverberate through history. There is a difference, however, between the speaking skills Chrysostom gave to the Christian tradition and the speaking of called men in the first century. That difference is not a fine line, but a vast gorge.

John Chrysostom—for better or for worse—left us with polished, professional pulpiteerism, a far cry from the New Testament business of prophetic utterance. Modern sermonics, homiletics, hermeneutics, rhetoric, oratory, and all related fields find their origins not in the first century prophets, but in the Graeco-Roman tradition of rhetoric. (Rhetoric is the structure and style of what you say.) Then, it was a rhetorical gift. Today, it's platform science. For instance, seminaries today teach us that the ideal sermon has an introduction, three memorable main points, and a conclusion. That's exactly what Aristotle said in his *Rhetoric* (no coincidence). A good sermon in a seminary classroom is a brilliant, well-thought-out message that flows from the mind; a good "sermon" around a kitchen table in A.D. 100 was a brief but sound message that flowed from the heart *and sprang from the situation at hand* rather than being etched in marble beforehand.

In his early pagan years, Chrysostom was a student of rhetoric. In fact, he was the most promising young orator in the Empire. His name, Chrysostom, means Golden-Mouth.

Then he got saved and ended up as the spellbinding bishop of the church in Antioch. History has judged him to be both courageous and foolhardy—and an egomaniac. *He and two or three other orators-turned-Christian-pulpiteers caused the Greek oratorical skills to replace the Judaeo-Christian practice of the prophet.* As a result, today we have an awful lot of pulpit pros, while the old-fashioned, free-speaking prophet has become an endangered species.

What we hear on Sunday morning is in the tradition of Greek orators and not in the lineage of the church planters, men like Peter—or Paul of Tarsus—with their fierce, bold proclamation of the gospel in marketplaces and open homes.

Such Hebrew preachers spoke sporadically, as prompted by the Holy Spirit. We get our preaching today every Sunday between 11:25 and 11:59, Holy Spirit or no.

They spoke extemporaneously, with little or no formal speech training. Someday you and I may be *forced* to abandon our polished platform rhetoric and follow their pattern—when the Scripture is fulfilled:

> When you are brought before synagogues, rulers and authorities, do not worry about how you will defend yourselves or what you will say, for the Holy Spirit will teach you in that very hour what you should say. (Luke 12:11-12)

The Church That Didn't Like Titles

What was church life like from A.D. 100 to 323?

The question is important because the closer you can get to those original Biblical patterns of a participatory church, the closer you'll be to having a happy, lively fellowship of believers.

Unfortunately, I have to tell you that we don't have a lot of direct descriptions of church life in that period. They're rare.

But we do have some things. Most notably, we have a vast array of random letters. Counting all types of written documents and correspondence, archeologists have about 500,000 specimens from this era, with about 25,000 of them categorized as "Christian" or "probably Christian." That means these documents make reference to church events, Christian concepts, etc. And here's the mind-blowing discovery they've made: *Not one of these 25,000 pieces of papyrus, etc., makes any reference to a clergyman. There is absolutely no mention of a "minister" or "priest" or "pastor" or any other term for any office or any kind of leadership.*

The leaders did exist, but their role certainly didn't fill up any space in the brains of the believers who wrote the letters! Or their lives! *To the early Christian, his church elder (bishop) was a "regular guy" who was an integral "part of the family," not a member of a special class that was <u>ever, ever</u> referred to by a title!*[17]

---

17. Incidentally, although most Romans had three or four names, Christians refused to use even their family surnames. It sounded too conceited and prideful to them. It gave away their standing in society. Using only first names, slaves and rich people could be on the same level, an arrangement that astounded outsiders!

Science Upsets the Rotten-Apple Cart

What about archeological documents after A.D. 330? After that date, they are replete with references to titles! But there's one big difference: Most of the surviving literature after 330 was penned by pagan philosophers-turned-Christian. Although their hearts had latched onto Jesus Christ, their minds made a slower transition. Nonetheless, they took it upon themselves to write philosophical and theological treatises on just about everything imaginable, and they tell us very little that is useful—and even less that's reliable—about *church life*. What church life looked like after 330 virtually never comes up as a subject. Most everything left to us seems to be literature by ex-pagan philosophers dueling with pagan philosophers!

A study of many such writers will give you a very mistaken impression of what church life was like. Their half-pagan, neo-Christian descent into philosophical nothingism is mind-boggling. Unfortunately, when you read these volumes (and almost nothing else has survived), you come away with the impression that all Christians were caught up in a philosophical, theological, and intellectual study in abstract tedium!

That is not so, of course. If today all Christian writings on earth burned in an atomic holocaust except for one library full of scholarly theology, a thousand years from now, people might think that today's Sunday schools and church socials consisted of normal families sitting around and philosophizing about millennial eschatology, process theology, situation ethics, infralapsarianism, and other academic chewing gum.

It looked for awhile like we would forever have to live with the distorted perspective that the church of that era was made up 100% of erudite theologians! Make no mistake, those men's writings are held in highest esteem, despite the fact that every one of them wrote from a solidly Socratic-Platonic-Aristotelian perspective.

So what did early Christianity actually look like after you peel off the accumulated layers of Ambrose, Gregory, Augustine, Tertullian, Jerome, Origen, and a few hundred others? Until 1989, you couldn't have known (unless you spoke French and happened to know about the one and only book on the subject).

Hold on to your hat. Modern archeology has very recently come up with a whole potful of fascinating, if not downright unbelievable, discoveries. To understand just how astonishing these findings are, and how contrary to all past interpretations of this era they are, we need to note a fact or two about Christian archeology itself.

A Trip Through the Catacombs

Modern Christian archeology was launched by Roman Catholic scholars about 1630.

They "got there first," and until recently their interpretation of the evidence left to us in literature, documents, and objects has been *the* accepted interpretation. And naturally, their interpretations were filtered through the mindset of Roman Catholic theologians. These men saw everything they looked at as reinforcing the Catholic view of the church.

Unfortunately (and incredibly), when Protestant archeology and even evangelical archeology emerged, they bought into these Catholic interpretations without question—and even taught them. The view of church history (A.D. 100 to 280) passed on even in our best seminaries was that of a church elaborate in ritual, with a powerful and well-defined clergy and a prescribed liturgy. It was a scenario that made the believers of that time look terribly religious, pious, and ascetic. We were taught that a distinct, powerful clergy overlorded virtually everything.

I came face to face with the Roman school of archeology just after finishing my first year in seminary at Ruschlikon, Switzerland. I spent that summer in Rome, and I was privileged to be able to get a personal guided tour of the catacombs by a priest versed in the history of the catacombs. We took candles and descended into that fantastic labyrinth. Along the way, he pointed out the Christian graffiti left on the walls, allegedly during the middle and late 200s and early 300s.

At one place he pointed to a Latin inscription and said, "This is early second century." With horror, I read the inscription: "Peter and Paul, pray for us." Every instinct in me rebelled. I just *knew* the statement scribbled on the ceiling of that underground trench was not part of the mind-set of second-century Christians.

Recent redating of this graffiti puts that very inscription after the Constantine era.

What we were being told was this: The second, third and fourth centuries were as full of ritual, clergy, liturgy, sobriety, austerity, pomp, and sacerdotalism as the fifth, sixth and seventh. That interpretation buttressed Roman Catholicism mightily, and the Protestants, blushing with embarrassment at such Catholic one-upmanship, could only mumble sadly, "Well, after A.D. 100 there was a great falling away of the faith."

And when Protestants themselves get tied up in pomp, ritual and clerical rule, they even point to the practices ascribed to the second and third century church. After all, it appears that it was doing nicely even though it was full of formality and dominated by an active ministry and a silent laity.

Well, it's not so. During the last decade archaeologists have been turning up new and revolutionary findings which have caused the archeological community to begin, for the first time, to re-examine past interpretations of known data. What has emerged is nothing less than stunning.

Some of the recent archaeologists who have been instrumental in the complete reinterpretation of second century Christianity are evangelical, others are liberal; but the conclusions are the same.[18] First of all, this new, emerging school is far more honest and scientific than was the Roman school. Secondly, it is working with far more data. Thirdly, these men are not taking their cue from Augustine, Ambrose, etc. As one scholar recently wrote in the Chicago Seminary Theological Review: "Trying to find out what the early church was like by studying the theologians of the second, third and fourth centuries would be the same thing as someone five thousand years from now reading nothing but the writings of Barth, Tillich and Neibuhr, and drawing from their writings a picture of what twentieth-century Christianity was like." (There is virtually nothing in these men's writings that describes what the church is like today.)

No Church Buildings

What has been discovered? Let's begin with Christian architecture—that is, church buildings.

The Roman school declared that church buildings have been with us from the second century on. It further taught that the church buildings erected during the Constantinian era were built on the sites of previous church structures. This dogma was universally accepted as fact.

But recently, Christian archeology has gone back to reinvestigate those sites. The findings: *Without exception, there was no church building or any other kind of Christian meeting place to be found*

---

18. Almost all of these scholars are French or German. We English-speakers are too busy digging up Old Testament ruins in Israel!

buried beneath any Constantinian-era church buildings. Archaeologists found either virgin land or pagan temples or marketplaces or maybe even an occasional Pizza Hut, but no evidence anywhere of any kind of building used for Christian gatherings.

The implications were staggering—and still are! They are a call to the whole church, Catholic and Protestant, to rethink the nature of what we call "church."

In one way, the most remarkable discovery was that of a single Christian meeting place—the only one ever found from the pre-Constantine era! Even it was not a church building, but a home that had been converted into a meeting place for Christians. The site is a town in Syria with the odd name of Duro-Europa.

Exhaustive studies have been made of this building. The upshot is this: It was just a home used in the mid-200s as a place for Christians to gather. One of its peculiarities: A wall had been torn out between two bedrooms to make one large room that would hold about seventy-five people sitting on the floor.

The point? Until Constantine, there was no such thing as a church building or "Christian" architecture. A church building had never been dreamed of in a dream. **That which we know as the Christian faith was a living room movement! The Christian faith was the first and only religion ever to exist that did not use special temples of worship; it is the only "living room" religion in human history.**

House Churches in Africa

Let's look at yet another surprising archeological find.

Imagine, if you will, a group of Christian archaeologists plowing their way through thousands of deeds and property records of towns and cities in North Africa. These deeds, surveys, title changes and tax records all dated from A.D. 100 to 400, and often stated the uses being made of each building.

Some of these documents tell the name of the family that lived in each house, the occupation of those employed, and their religion. Some of these records also tell what other activities the building was used for besides living quarters. ("Baking located here"; "Pots made here," etc.) Lo and behold, from time to time notations are found that say, essentially, "The Christian ecclesia sometimes holds meetings in this house"!

Exciting? Well, on some occasions archaeologists have been able to locate these very sites and do a dig. The invariable findings: an ordinary house. No more, no less. All scientific evidence of this era rises up to declare to us that the Christian faith was utterly informal in its expression, and homes were its base!

A formalized Christianity in a ceremonial setting was invented during and immediately after the age of Constantine. *It did not grow out of a slow, natural progression to a more mature church, but out of a sudden captivity to a half-converted, neo-pagan worldview.* **The institutionalization of the church was not a step up, but a step off the precipice into a chasm of slavery to unbiblical traditions.**

We are still in that chasm. Your own church may be as orthodox as sunshine in July, but chances are that 50% to 90% of its *practices* are hand-me-downs from Mr. Constantine. Small wonder that noted Temple University historian Franklin Littell calls Constantine, "that great whale that broke the net."

Christian Art

Early Christian stonework and carvings have now presented us with yet another surprise.

At some point in your cultural upbringing, you may have groaned your way through a museum full of old Christian art. You saw painting after painting of fat baby Jesuses with sallow-faced Marys, and sickly, tragic-looking Jesuses with the trademark halo and the hands held just so—all of which were codified and required by rigid convention.

What makes these works even more depressing is that you and I have been told that no matter how far back we go, Christian art *always* looked about like this. Well, that's just not so—and now we have the research to prove it.

The old Roman school of archeology dated almost all of the dreary, miserable-looking stonework, carving, and other artifacts quite early. But a more enlightened and unprejudiced dating has now been able to divide these findings into four groups: (1) early; (2) just prior to Constantine; (3) the Constantinian era; and (4) the post-Constantine era.

Generally speaking, here is what emerges. In groups one and two, you see depicted happy crowds of people following a joyful, charismatic, and itinerant Lord. In the post-Constantinian era, you see a sober, grave, unhappy, austere Christ sitting on a throne, garbed in the robes of a Caesar with bolts of lightning breaking around Him.

Two points: First, men tend to depict in art what they see in their minds. *A radical and terrible change in the minds of Christians as to what Christ was like and what a Christian should look like had taken place in less than seventy years.* Second, powerful men seeking total power *had* to depict a *ruling* Savior to justify their *own* rule. A poor, itinerant model would not do.

One of the most telling proofs of the enormous change that occurred at that point in time is found in those artworks depicting the Lord's Supper. Incredibly, early Christian art that has to do with the Lord's Supper *never* depicts the night before the crucifixion, but rather shows the Lord feeding the five thousand! The early artists saw the Lord's Supper as a time of joy, with the Lord providing for five thousand of His people. Later you find depicted a dismal Christ in the upper room staring morbidly at a cup, with the dozen around him sober-faced and sad.

Which do you think reflects the first-century mind? And which do you think depicts our present attitude toward the Lord's Supper?

In conclusion, most of our heritage of "Christian practices" in today's Protestant church is not legitimate. The doctrine is correct, the rest of the Christian picture is not. When Protestants left the Catholic church, they did not leave behind everything that was in error.

It's time to face the facts: You and I have been sold a bill of goods.

7
Luther Quit Too Soon

by Gene Edwards
with banter and counterpoint by James Rutz

The Reformation was made possible by one man. And it wasn't Luther.

It also wasn't Zwingli or Hus or Wycliffe or Calvin or Hobbes.

The credit goes to Frederick the Wise, without whom Dr. Luther would have been turned into a little pile of carbon by age 34, if not earlier.

Frederick the Wise, alias Frederick III, just happened to command the largest army in Europe, and he was royally peeved because he had not been made Pope. In fact, there was a lot of unrest all across northern (non-Latin) Europe over the behavior of the Roman Catholic Church hierarchy down in Italy.

Now, in Saxony, where Frederick ruled, there was this perfectly delightful, beer-loving German monk who taught Augustinian theology at the University of Wittenberg. And he was *really* upset with the church.

Luther's conduct and writings were reprehensible to the Roman Catholic Church, and normally he would have been put on trial as a heretic and burned alive. But Prince Frederick, bless his heart, took a shine to Luther, and decided to give protection to the Germanic radical. Essentially what Frederick said was, "Let that man say what he has to say; let no one touch him." And no one else had an army big enough to argue with him.

If you do not understand Frederick the Wise's army, you do not understand the Reformation. Catholic malcontents had been around for centuries. The key to the Reformation's success was not some great spiritual revival, but the military might of Frederick (who, ironically, probably remained a Catholic to the end).

The final outcome of this was that the land of Saxony removed Roman Catholicism as its official state religion (the first nation ever to do so). To fill this vacuum, Luther was given free rein to establish a whole new state religion from the ground up!

That brings us to the era where we picked up the lion's share of Protestant practices.

Luther had before him a nation filled with empty, ex-Roman Catholic church buildings. He sent his followers out to man these church buildings and to promulgate his teachings to the faithful. Earlier, many Catholic priests had read Luther's writings and had left the Catholic ministry. Most got married, and many came to Luther's home seeking teaching and direction. (He performed no small number of marriages between ex-priests and ex-nuns, and ordained a host of "Lutheran" ministers.)

During these incredible times, Luther produced an entire ecclesiastical structure out of bare bones, created a flood of Lutheran literature and got it distributed. He single-handedly created a Protestant catechism for children, a Protestant hymn book, and a Protestant Bible, which he translated, published and distributed.

While doing all this, he taught and trained ex-priests to become Lutheran ministers and Bible expositors. Wherever possible, he was sending these men out to serve as Protestant ministers to those empty church buildings all over Saxony.

Those Lutheran ministers were looked upon as a Protestant version of a priest. Up until that time the "pastoral role," the pastoral practice of the Protestant world, did not exist. The modern-day pastoral concept began in Wittenberg, Germany. So did a lot of our other "New Testament practices." Here is the story of Wittenberg.

The Great Pulpit Switch

Luther had the entire altar area ripped out of the front of the church where he spoke.

High up on one of the pillars of the church was a little rostrum, or pulpit, which the Catholic priest had climbed up to by means of a circular staircase to read dutifully the weekly announcements to the faithful flock below. (If you're ever visiting a "tourist cathedral" and there's no one around, you have my permission to sneak up into the pulpit and look down, imagining you're addressing a full house of upturned faces. If your circuitry is anything like normal, you will experience an enormous, almost dizzying sense of power.)

Luther had one of those high pulpits placed in the front and center of the church building where the altar had been. That was new. Brand new. And so, dear reader, was born the mighty Protestant pulpit. A step in the right direction, definitely—but still a device that centralized and monopolized sharing and communication, leaving it strictly in the hands of paid employees with professional training—while we sit silently in the pews.

What's So Special About 11 A.M.?

Luther faithfully preached every Sunday at dawn. The hour was exactly the same that Catholic mass had been scheduled for eons.

Luther, however, did *not* enjoy getting up that early. (Night owls, take comfort!)

What he really preferred was to go down to the tavern—or sit in his kitchen—and talk theology with his friends and drink beer on Saturday night. In fact, the tune of his famous hymn, "A Mighty Fortress Is Our God," was a popular German drinking song of his day. (Even if you don't drink, you just *gotta* love a guy like that!)

So, before long, he moved the Protestant worship service to the saner hour of 9 A.M.—though not without sustaining numerous complaints from the early bird faction.

But the older he got, the longer he gabbed on Saturday night and the more beer he drank. He moved the service to 10 A.M.—to the tune of more complaints.

But as he talked still longer, he found even 10 A.M. to be uncomfortably early. The last possible hour he could set for the service and still call it "morning worship" was 11 A.M. So he did. And that is how it came about that 500,000,000 Protestants today hold church services every Sunday at *11 A.M.!*

So the next time you roll over and catch up on your sleep on a Sunday morning, remember to thank the Lord for Martin Luther and his endless late-night Bierfests.

Luther and the Hymn Sandwich

Luther also set in concrete the order of worship you'll probably follow next Sunday morning. (He may have adapted Calvin's version of the Sunday morning worship service. It's a moot question.

Calvin and Luther both invented their Sunday morning rituals about 1540, and the two are virtually identical.)

He set the Protestant ritual for Wittenberg and, with only the slightest variations, we all follow that same liturgy today. Regardless of our denomination, across the face of the entire planet, we copy the immutable, sacrosanct order handed to us down through the ages ... at 11 A.M., of course ...

- Opening Song
- Prayer
- Three Songs
- Announcements[19]
- Prayer
- Offertory
- Song
- Sermon
- Benediction

The Golden Arches have flourished worldwide, largely for one reason: You can go into any McDonald's anywhere, and you know *exactly* what you'll get, right down to a few thousandths of a pound. Luther's hymn sandwich, like the Big Mac, also thrives on predictability. It's the same week after week, month after month, year after year, decade after decade, generation after generation, world without end, amen.

Seminaries and Fig Leaves, the Counter Reformation's Whitewash

The Council of Trent was called by the Pope in 1545 to answer the question, "What are we going to do about this fellow Luther?"

With a little more humility, they might have figured out that their doctrine had gone somewhat astray over the centuries. But no, they refused to admit that until much later.

They decided the problems the Catholic church had were twofold: (1) their priests were not well educated and (2) the reason for all the immorality in the priesthood *and* among the laity was all those nude statues and paintings created during the Renaissance.

To solve the first problem, they invented the theological seminary, something unknown for the previous fifteen centuries. To solve the

---

19. We Baptists spend about ten minutes making announcements. I'm not sure whether that's worse or better than the Lutherans, Presbyterians, etc.

second, in 1564 they sent out squads of amused artisans armed with plaster of Paris from which they fashioned history's first fig leaves to cover up the obvious source of all their morality problems.

And now sometimes, on a moonlit night when sleep evades my worried brow, I lie in bed and wonder, "How could this old earth have survived without seminaries and fig leaves? What would life be like without them?" It's worth at least a ponder.

Denominations and the Fixation on Doctrine

Over the centuries, movements and denominations have split off and set up shop by the tens of thousands—mostly for fleshly reasons.

But in today's mobile societies, people choose a denomination mostly for reasons of *psychological fit.* There are three types of Christians: thinkers, feelers, and doers. And we have denominations custom-made for each.

- The thinkers want the feelers to get logical.
- The feelers want the thinkers to lighten up and smell the roses.
- The doers want both types to get in gear and start evangelizing.
- The feelers just want to be left alone to love God, chase moonbeams, read poetry, perform miracles, see signs, get power, and watch sunsets. (I may be exaggerating a tad here for clarity.)

Long before there were Protestants, the Catholic Church tried to make room under one umbrella for all three types, with philosophy and theology for the *thinkers*, missions and monkships for the *doers*. They had an off-and-on admiration for the feelers (punctuated with periods of banishment, imprisonment, and burning at the stake—courtesy of the thinkers).

Then along came Luther (a doctor of theology, a student of Augustine's philosophy, an Augustine monk, etc.). He often declared that those Catholic feelers (the Catholics called them "mystics") would *never* gain a toehold in his Lutheran world. Consequently, the Reformation was primarily a *theological and intellectual* movement. It was woefully lacking as a revolution of spiritual maturity and lacked in giving people a practical grasp on a deeper walk with the Lord. The early Protestants hardly even made a dent in having a deeper walk with Christ.

Since that time, Europe has fought hundreds of wars over doctrinal disputes. Millions have been killed, and precious few of the fatalities have been caused by missionaries or moonbeam chasers. The bloodshed came from the intellectual, rational, logical, doctrinal differences of the thinkers.

Sometime you might find it interesting to read about, say, the Huguenots—just to pick one example out of many. Read about them in dungeons, tied on racks, being roasted over fires, molten lead poured in their mouths, eyes gouged out, women in birth pangs with their legs tied together while mother and child died in unbelievable agony. In each case, a theologian stood beside them, Bible in hand, to convince the tortured Huguenot that the *intelligent* thing to do would be to recant.[20] And still we pass down through the generations the non-scriptural slogan, "Don't trust your feelings."[21] At least you shouldn't trust thinkers any more than you do feelers.

Today we have 23,000 denominations, each with its own pet doctrines, the logical offspring of the Reformation. God in Heaven, please forgive us.

Stained Glass, Steeples, and Vaulted Ceilings

As of this date, there are probably fewer than 200 Protestants in the world who know the facts that follow.

I will greatly condense an exceedingly complex story that took me many years to uncover and led me on a long, demanding trek from Sophia to Rome to the stacks of the UCLA library.

Let's begin here: Stained glass windows, steeples, and high vaulted church ceilings got into our lives through Plato, not Christ. Plato wrote again and again about light and space and color as they relate to man's upward spiritual striving toward the "unknowable" Divine essence, the "other than," the "touch with the sublime," the "moment of awe."

The early Christians knew that God could be known, that we could meet Him directly, heart to heart, right here and now. In a different sense, we also meet Him in face-to-face, down-to-earth fellowship with other believers. The early Christians saw no need for stained glass and steeples to point us upward to a God just out of reach. **He**

---

20. If you read about the Huguenots, you will read almost alone. A few years ago, the French government issued a postage stamp proudly proclaiming, "1685-1985: France Welcomes the Huguenots." A red-faced French post office quickly withdrew the stamp when someone pointed out that 1685 was the year when whole provinces emptied as countless Huguenots, under severe persecution, fled abroad in every direction. —J.R.

21. As Jack Hayford once observed, "What does that mean? That our minds are flawless?" —J.R.

is here! they said. **He is among us!** But walk into any cathedral, and you will immediately be staring upward toward an unreachable apex in the sanctuary. *Permanent awe, permanent frustration.*

Plato insisted that man must go through a number of ascensions and plateaus to meet the divine essence. It takes a lifetime, he warned, and very few will achieve it. Only the gifted will succeed, and that through much suffering. The Catholics adopted the Platonic "Stages of Ascent." They can be found in virtually all their writings on the subject of knowing God.

Plato's brilliant nonsense was enthusiastically picked up, massaged, endorsed, and passed on down by generations of heavy-duty Christian thinkers like Origen, and Augustine. They gradually fine-tuned Plato's thoughts into a formidable worldview called *religious Neo-Platonic Dualism.*

Now, we could have survived this empty philosophizing pretty easily except for one thing: a nameless, one-man disaster team from Syria, a truly warped monk of about A.D. 500 who called himself...

DIONYSIUS THE AREOPAGITE   Pseudo-Dionysius, as he is called today, was a prolific author—and a total fraud. He claimed that his writings were those of the *original* Dionysius, a real disciple who actually did live in first century Greece and was led to Christ by St. Paul (Acts 17:34). (Pseudo-Dionysius also claimed that Timothy had sat at his own feet. Pretty good for a monk writing in A.D. 500 about events in A.D. 50!)

This rascal was enamored of Neo-Platonic philosophy, which was in vogue then. When people read his writings, they really thought they were listening to a profound Christian who was a personal friend and student of Paul. So they thought Paul was a Neo-Platonic philosopher-theologian, too!

It was nearly a thousand years before this hoax was finally rejected. By then the damage was done, and it was *irreversible.* **This man's ideas are warp and woof of Christian thought, and will remain so until the Lord returns.** Why? Because his brand of philosophy was picked up and integrated into our intellectual heritage by every Christian thinker for a whole millennium—including, alas, a fellow named...

ABBOTT SUGER   Suger (soo-ZHAY) was the head of France's national church in St. Denis (de-NEE) from 1122 to 1151. (Denis is the patron saint of France.)

Now back before 825, there had been this fable that Dionysius of

Syria (500) was the Dionysius of A.D. 50. Unfortunately for all of us, there had been a Christian missionary killed in France in 250 named Denis. The village of St. Denis grew up on that spot. In 825, someone at the church in St. Denis made the astonishing claim that the Dionysius of A.D. 50, the Denis of 250, and the Dionysius of 500 were *all the same guy!* Which guy? The convert of Paul, of course. And everyone believed the story! The writings of Pseudo-Dionysius now became just about the most important documents in Christian history, and in the process this fable made Paul a follower of Plato. Read it and weep!

Suger jumped on this legend, and in 1140 created the world's first Gothic cathedral—and the Christian theology of architecture. He deliberately emphasized light, space, color, man's littleness, God's greatness and His "other-than unknowableness." Suger *proved* this was Christian—and St. Paul's view—by quoting Dionysius!! (He had to overcome the objections of Bernard of Clairvaux, the famous ascetic who was his boss—and who didn't want to build it at *all*.)

Church architecture as philosophy and theology has been with us ever since. Stained glass windows (light), high ceilings, vaults and arches (awe, wonder, the littleness of man, the greatness of God) all combined to produce a spiritual experience by physical means. Walk into any cathedral, and you will understand. (You'll also *whisper*—no matter how hard you try not to.) The touch of the sublime, the sense of awe! All of this is of body and soul, no part of it is of the spirit.

Even worse, Pseudo-Dionysius' fantasies were lionized by the most important Christian thinker since Paul...

THOMAS AQUINAS Imagine a mind great enough to integrate Augustine with the other early Christian writings; harmonize Plato, Aristotle, and the Neo-Platonists; then combine them all into one massive system of thought ... called New Testament theology!

This is exactly what Thomas Aquinas did in his *Summa Theologica* before he died in 1274. Thomistic thought is so brilliant that it is still the *official* doctrine of the Catholic church seven centuries later.

You're not Catholic? No matter. Attend virtually any Protestant seminary in the world, you will still be taught from books that follow his format and from lesson plans that mimic his line of thought. And when you go out to preach, you will preach Christ **and** Aquinas (which includes huge doses of Pseudo-Dionysius because Aquinas quoted that wretch *over 100 times* in his *Summa*.) It's a package deal. It's not even a salad you can pick over with a fork, but a systematic stew.

If you read Western man's best thoughts about God, you also get

Parmenides, Anaxagoras, Heraclitus, Pythagoras, Antisthenes, Zeno of Citium, Panaetius, Sation, Seneca, Epictetus, Socrates, Plato, Aristotle, Philo, the stoics, Plotinus, Clement, Numenius, Origen, Augustine, Speusippus, Arcesilaus, Carneades, the skepticism of the Academies, Saccas, Tertullian, Aquinas, and—lucky you—a little bit of St. Paul.

After Constantine, the understanding of our faith quickly fell into the hands of big-time intellectual speculators. And no one noticed that the church was losing spiritual depth in quantities exactly equal to its gains in profound philosophy. The intellectual leadership of Christianity soon became the property of some very brainy gentlemen who spoke and theorized somewhere out above the upper stratosphere of the outer ectoplasm—at the expense of ordinary working blokes like you and me, who would gladly settle for a few good thoughts on how to get through the week.

Why You Wear Your Sunday Best

Why did Christians start dressing up to go to church?

If you've ever yanked a tie tightly around your sweaty neck on a hot, steaming day—or ouched your way to church in a pair of not-quite-fitting high heels, you may have said to yourself, "I'd sure like to meet the dirty dog who invented these things ... in a dark alley."

Actually, you're probably under the impression that dressing up for church is a godly custom designed to show our respect for the Lord. It's not. While showing respect for God is always good, that's just not the historical reason for shined shoes, fresh shirts, and attention to style.

Nor do we dress to impress each other—although many people do find it uplifting to be among well-turned-out friends.

History is a little fuzzy on this, but as near as anyone can tell, the real reason for our Sunday splendor is so that we'll look good if we happen to run into Emperor Constantine or his aristocratic friends!

Chances for that are not high these days, but originally that was the reason. Constantine and other heavy hitters had a habit of popping up in several of the church buildings he paid for. And when big cathedrals sprang up much later, with European royalty in attendence, the impetus to dress up grew further. Fancy church buildings were the one place that royalty mixed with commoners. Cathedrals, such as those at St. Denis, attracted royalty from all over, and it simply wouldn't <u>do</u> to bump into a prince or contessa in your grubby work clothes.

These are just historical observations, of course. I wouldn't be so foolish as to question the advisability of an ages-old custom like dressing up for church. If snappy clothing brings you closer to God, helps you deal humbly with sin in your life, lets you relax and get your eyes on Christ while feeling closer to your brothers and sisters in church, why, I'm all for it. In fact, maybe I'll join you ... just as soon as I can locate my Christian Dior cravat and Yves Saint Laurent silk suit.

And Speaking of Clothes...

The clerical "backwards collar" deserves to be awarded a small note here.

At one brief point in European history, every man who could afford a suit had a shirt or two with a reverse collar. It was simply the style *du jour.*

Eventually, however, it went the way of all styles, and no one wore it any more—except, that is, for the clergy. Being perpetually underpaid, ministers and missionaries have never been noted for up-to-the-minute fashions. And in this particular case, they continued to wear the now-venerable reverse collar simply because they didn't have the money to refurbish their wardrobes with newer shirts.

And Now, Direct from Luther's Kitchen, We Bring You: *The New Professional Pastorate*

The Protestant Reformation was primarily a doctrinal, intellectual, and ecclesiastical event.

People did get saved and lives were changed. Praise God for every one. But love of the brethren was not the keynote. The Reformation set the foundation for the great evangelical, fundamental, and charismatic movements of the last 200 years, and yet it was lacking in many practical aspects. For one example, the Catholics were sending out far more missionaries than the early Lutherans ever thought about. So when Catholicism lost half of Europe during the Reformation, it still grew in size because of its missionaries going out all over the world. Missions had not even been born among Protestants— and would not be for another 250 years. We stole half of Europe by force and then didn't grow an inch!

The Reformation was also a time of accumulating traditions— which evolved straight out of the circumstances of the hour. One of these was the modern day pastoral role.

Now, imagine a nation full of empty church buildings. Then imagine Wittenberg looking something like a refugee camp. Ex-priests and ex-nuns were pouring in literally by the ox cart load! From all over Europe, men who had read Luther's writing were moving to Wittenberg to sit at his feet. Luther, in turn, was training, speaking, and writing volumes, and working to fill those empty church buildings with Protestant ministers as fast as he could.

Those converted ex-priests from Wittenberg were (1) following Luther's teachings, (2) taking off their priestly robes,[22] (3) getting married to ex-nuns, (4) setting up new pulpits where the Eucharist was once located, and (5) preaching the Word every Sunday morning at 11 A.M.

Until that time, communities were accustomed to having priests in their city who were carrying out *the seven pastoral duties of a priest*. They were used to seeing them:

1. marry the young
2. bury the dead
3. hear confession
4. bless community events
5. baptize their babies
6. visit the sick, and
7. care for and collect money for the poor and the church.

Remember, these were the pastoral duties of *Catholic* priests that had come into being over a thousand year period of tradition and evolution. (In other words, these customs had little to do with the Bible.)

Now, Luther instructed these men to continue the pastoral duties of a priest—with only a tiny alteration. He changed one particular Catholic duty, that of "hearing confessions." This gave way, thankfully, to spiritual counsel and preaching the Bible. In light of Luther's thundering theological revolution, his minuscule changes in ministry may seem strange to us, but every generation is subject to its matrix. *Luther simply could not think of a more scriptural job description for his fleet of professional pastors than that of a not-quite-*

---

22. Incidentally, reformer John Calvin determined he would *not* wear priestly robes. As a protest to the costumed pageantry of other clergy, he stuck to his business suit for even the most formal church occasions. But alas, his followers through the ages have also worn a business suit—*exact copies of Calvin's business suit.* And thus today, when you see a Presbyterian minister in full regalia, you are looking at a sixteenth century Swiss Brooks Brothers' boardroom special. —J.R.

Catholic priest! So was born the practice of the modern day pastor.

Also, tragically, Luther felt that the laymen around him were so backward, illiterate, and ill-prepared to minister that he was afraid to move ahead to the next logical step of restoring open worship, sharing, and lay ministry. Writing of the sort of laymen he would need, he said, "I cannot find them."

The CEO/Pastor in the Bible

The modern concept of the pastor grew out of Wittenberg, Germany, and was but an adaptation of the pastoral duties of a priest! If you aren't shocked, you sure ought to be.

From that day on, people have written literally millions of books on every theological issue conceivable to the mind of man, yet almost no one has closely questioned the Biblical basis for the all-in-one pastor, a man who operates as the heart and soul of the church. He is just there. I repeat, he was not born as a result of profound scriptural study. The modern pastor just grew like Topsy out of the swirl of events in Wittenberg between 1525 and 1540. Before that the present Protestant pastor never existed, nor was he ever dreamed of.

In all of the millions of debates in church history, there has not been so much as one day of controversy over his scriptural right to exist! Yet there is not one verse of Scripture in the New Testament that describes such a creature, and only one verse that even uses the term "pastors" (Ephesians 4:11). Nonetheless, he is the center of the practice of Protestant Christianity.[23]

One of the most fascinating things about the modern day practice of the CEO/pastor is that ministers seem to know—or sense—that their job is non-scriptural. As a pastor, then later as an evangelist, and until

---

23. I feel that the problem is not in having a pastor, for pastor-equippers are scriptural. The problems are:

1. Dividing up the body of Christ into two parts: overworked leaders and sedentary serfs.

2. Putting up a nearly unscalable wall between the two.

3. Convincing the laity that it's OK to sit back and relinquish their freedom, their authority, their ministries, their intimacy with other believers, their priesthood before God, etc., etc.

4. Making a pastor into an unscriptural chief executive officer/church president/ administrator/errand boy for laymen who don't want to visit the sick, etc./head counselor/permanent pulpit fixture/chief cook and bottle washer/neo-priest straight out of the Roman tradition. —J.R.

this very hour, I have brought up this question to scores of fellow ministers: "Where is the present day practice of a pastor found in Scripture? I cannot find it." *The most reaction I have ever received was either agreement or a resigned shrug! No honest pastor will defend the role of today's pastorate in light of the New Testament.*[24]

Today's version of Protestantism rests on the concept and practice of the pastor, but he exists nowhere in New Testament Scripture. Yet ironically, he's the fellow we hire and put in the pulpit to call us all to be faithful to the Bible! *O Consistency, where are thy children?*[25]

Snapshots of a CEO/Pastor's Life

I'm throwing in this extra little section at no additional charge. Call it "the confessions of a minister who never got a handle on how to be a pastor"!

The snapshots below are to show you how the theoretical problems of an unscriptural pastorate have real-life consequences....

1. "Ladies and gentlemen, this evening we are gathered together to see the hockey team from Montreal get out here and murder the hockey team from Seattle. They're going to beat one another senseless with clubs and sticks and knock one another over and hit each other. Also there will be riots in the stands. But just before that happens, we're going to have the pastor of the First Baptist Church come and lead us in prayer."

(Have you ever tried to think up a prayer for two groups of men who are about to kill one another over a hockey puck?)

---

24. If he does, he has to find (1) one pastoral man burying people with an oration given over the corpse, (2) one man preaching a sermon on Sunday, (3) one man visiting the sick, (4) one man directing the church, saleried, and subject to the whims of the congregation, (5) one man saying prayers over civic meetings and football games, (6) one man marrying the young, baptizing converts, and visiting the elderly, and (7) one man always dressed up in a suit. Try it! It can't be done!

25. Is the idea of a pastor a Protestant doctrine? If it is, I cannot find it. It seems to be only a practice, and has never been a doctrine. I am a graduate of the largest Protestant seminary in the world, which has on its campus one of the largest theological libraries ever assembled in the history of Christendom. I have searched that library for even one book or one chapter, and finally in desperation, even one paragraph which talks about a positive effort to show that there is something like today's pastoral concept in the New Testament. I have never found that book, nor chapter, nor page, nor paragraph on the subject. The CEO/pastor is just *there.* As far as I can discover no one has ever tried to prove the pastoral concept and practice as being Scriptural. Like the church parking lot, the CEO/pastor just **is.**

Kind of mind-boggling, isn't it?

2. The local businessmen's club is about to start ... amid chaos, noise, dirty jokes, swearing, bragging, and cocktails. Then the announcement: "Will Reverend Edwards please lead us in prayer?" And 1.001 seconds after the prayer, the carousing resumes.

But that pales in the presence of number three:

3. "Hello, pastor. Uncle Kurt died this morning. I'd like you to do his funeral Tuesday." ("Who is Uncle Kurt?" I wanted to ask!)

My reply: "Why, of course, sister. What time will it be?" (I have to say that. I'm a pastor. We alone bury the dead. I know: It's not in Scripture; it's a Catholic practice brought over from heathenism. Nonetheless, we Protestant preachers bury the dead. We dare not do otherwise!)

The reply I wanted to give: "I'm sorry, that just wouldn't be right. I never did know him very well, and for the life of me, I can't think of a single kind word to say about the old hypocrite. Let someone in your family do it. Let a neighbor do it. Preaching over the corpse of a man who may well be on his way down, not up, is something I refuse to do. Plus, funeral services are a holdover from Old Testament and pagan customs, anyway. Christians didn't even *have* funerals in New Testament times." (Burials and mourning, yes; funerals, no.)

Why didn't I say that? Because that reply would have won me first place in the unemployment line within 24 hours.

4. "The Democratic Party this evening is gathered to hear the Honorable Sam Squeak speak, and now will Reverend Edwards lead us in prayer?" Maybe Reverend Edwards is a Republican, but he still has to pray. Why? Because he is a pastor. That's what pastors do.

But even worse is number five:

5. The telephone rings, and a devout Sunday morning attendee says, "Pastor, my daughter wants to talk to Santa Claus. Be Santa Claus for my daughter. Here she is."

A little bitty voice asks, "Is this Santa Claus?" And for five minutes I play Santa Claus on the telephone. My salary of $55 a week and a parsonage depend on it!

How would you like to have to do things like this? And wear a suit at all times except in the shower or in bed? ... See your wife and kids subjected to constant, town-wide scrutiny? ... Never be allowed to be angry, depressed, short-tempered? ... Be required to talk piously all day long and do and say some of the most stupid things imaginable? It's all part of the job description. But it is not in the Scriptures.

There is not an honest man alive today in the ministry that has not wished to unload and drop this whole masquerade and be an ordinary human being. None of this tradition has anything to do with the Christian faith. In fact, the Christian faith stood *against* this kind of thing for the first few centuries.

But number six is the darkest snapshot of all!...

6. A conversation that is a blend of many true incidents: The telephone rings. "Hi, Pastor, this is Benedict. Pastor, my wife and I just want you to know that we love you so much."

"Thanks so much, Benedict. You're a fine person to say so. God love you, brother, for so thoughtful a nature."

"Pastor, we're going on vacation to the French Alps for the next month, and we have a country retreat house out on the lake. Lulu and I just wanted you to know that it's yours every week while we're gone. You can take your family out there, and rest and pray and enjoy it."

"Why, Benedict, that's the most gracious and Christian thing a person could do. God bless you, dear brother. My wife and I think so highly of you."

They both hang up. Each has—knowingly—"scratched the other's back."

Benedict feels all warm inside, knowing *God must love him because the pastor does.* The pastor hangs up knowing he has gotten something out of a layman by means of the scepter of religious blessing. It feels so good to both!

This kind of co-dependent relationship sometimes grows up between pastors and laymen (even poor ones) to the point it almost becomes a science. I, the pastor, bless you, the layman; that means God loves you. You, the layman, bless me (and buy God's favor) by giving me gifts, special attention, special meals—and sometimes a weekend retreat house. You, the layman, become a sycophant, treating me as someone special. And I, the pastor, use my sacred call from God for ego gratification or material gain. While this sort of thing goes on, reality lives in some other part of the world—and heaven weeps while hell chuckles.

Symbiotic relationships will continue as long as we have a rigid division between clergy and laity. Psychologically, in fact, this just might be the main reason we have a hired servant of God and an endowing laity: so that laymen can shirt tail into God's favor without doing all the heavy work and the man called of God can have a steady income. But whatever the cause, it needs to stop.

If open church life is ever to be widely known on earth, the whole mentality that spawned the modern CEO/pastor/priest role must go.

It demeans the layman and exalts the pastor—at the expense of God.[26]

What Is Left After the Shell Is Gone?

We could go on. We could get into Mr. Welch's successful campaign for grape juice, Karate for Christ classes, the Easter Bunny, Rudolph the Red-Nosed Reindeer, and much more.

But instead, let's gather up all these traditions we just looked at, all picked up from Constantine, the age of the Reformation, etc. (Remember, most Christians think all these things are based on the New Testament.) Put them together, and you pretty well have the whole of the practices of Protestantism. Remove this collateral luggage, and you remove most of what we Christians do and practice. There's just not much left!

Yet none of it has any root in Scripture. Every add-on item listed here can be traced back to its historical beginnings. All come *after* Constantine:

- church buildings
- church names
- pews
- sermons
- choirs
- the 11 A.M. starting time
- stained glass windows
- steeples
- high vaulted ceilings
- liturgies and rituals in church worship
- costumed clergy
- seminaries
- children named after "saints"
- dressing up for church
- denominations
- funerals
- the modern pastoral concept

---

26. If you want to hire a pastor to "equip your laymen for the work of the ministry," I think that's fine. Support him with all your heart as he transforms faltering believers and shows them how to be happy, fearless, loving giants of faith.

But if you hire a pastor and tell him to monopolize the communication in your meetings and you put in his hand the scepter of a Chief Executive Officer and Protestant priest, you're on your own when it comes to sorting out the resulting headaches and complications, which may be with you unto the third generation. —J.R.

• our fixation on doctrine to the exclusion of other matters.

I repeat, these practices all grew up in the post-apostolic period. Furthermore, most of them stand as a barrier to the restoration of a live encounter with Jesus Christ in church life. And they have been a barrier for the last seventeen hundred years. Yet they are very expensive to have. There is a price—in spirit, mind, and money—to keep the present-day church running.

This is a call for you and your church to make a clean break with Constantine and his whole pagan world. The time has arrived for us all to return to our roots, to the free, unspoiled, unregimented fellowship and worship that the family of the Lord Jesus Christ had for the first three centuries of her history.

Let's open up the church to everyone!

PART THREE

Five Ways to Open Your Church Without a Crowbar

Get ready for some pleasant surprises when you start talking about the open church. Many people will welcome you with open arms, like the Berliners welcomed the opening of the Wall.

Today, millions of believers *want* to be active participants in the life of the church, not just ecclesiastical barnacles. They're primed. They're ready. They're eager to be involved in pure worship, true sharing, and free ministry—if they only knew how.

Just prior to finishing this book, I self-published Part One of it as a four dollar minibook, *1700 Years Is Long Enough*. The response opened my eyes:

- Even though it wasn't sold in stores, people grabbed up twenty thousand copies in fifteen months. I had to reprint four times.
- The *average* buyer turned around and bought 2.4 more copies for his friends (unheard of in publishing, I'm told).
- Very, very few of the buyers were "young Turks" in their twenties. Most were heartsick pew-warmers in their fifties and sixties. But what really blew me away was that...
- *One-fourth of the buyers were pastors!* (Not a few of whom were burnout candidates looking for a better way to operate.)

And people wrote letters. Boy, did they ever.

I'd like for you to see a few typical responses. But first let me say that I'm not into patting myself on the back. In fact, I just can't stand gasbags who hype their own image. I do hope you understand I'm not trying to do that below. I simply want you to see how people feel so that you know they'll appreciate it when you talk to them about the open church.

I'll even put these letters in small type so you'll feel free to skim over them just for their general flavor:

You described exactly the way I have felt for so long. I had decided to quit the church I have been attending *the very day* I received this. It was like confirmation that I wasn't just an old fault-finder or wanting to be noticed. I go regularly, I tithe, and I try to be a part, but I feel unattached to the body. After spending many, many years being faithful and serving as a teacher, loving Jesus with all my heart and loving His people, it just doesn't seem right to be made to feel like a scattered sheep with no shepherd.
—M. R., Texas

My wife finally made me quit reading and come to bed late last night. Said I was making too much noise laughing and shouting, "This is great! Listen to this!" I finished it first thing this morning. Great! Tremendous! ... As pastor of a 39-year-old Southern Baptist Church, I'm committed to leading this church to become an open church. We've recently created a slot for spontaneous conversational praise-praying on Sunday morning. The body is catching on. We have trashed the printing of the "order of worship" for the congregation. (The leaders have one with the understanding that it is non-binding.) I must admit, however, that the changes in philosophy of worship and our commitment to stop "playing church" cost us four deacons and several families they influenced, who held an attitude of, "Do it my way or I'll take my marbles and go home." We hated to see them leave, but once you've experienced freedom, you don't want to go back into slavery.
—C.W., Louisiana

Thanks! We started open worship last Sunday and the response was fantastic! The people were very excited about it. And this is in a [conservative liturgical] Church! We were an older, dying church which had just about given up hope (I certainly had!) I was cautious—I wanted to slowly introduce the concept and "teach" people about it thru the summer. My elders got all fired up and said, "Why wait?" "Let's do it now!" So we did. I'm glad I listened to them and not the committee of seminary professors in my head.
—R.C., California

There is such dissatisfaction in the body of Christ no matter where you go. In conversation, we and others have said the same things you spoke out on. People are aware, and they're ready for a change.
—J.S., Kansas

Praise God! For the last fifteen years I have studied, wondered and prayed about this very thing: the priesthood of all believers. This is a great confirmation and encouragement to me [as a pastor] to know that God is speaking this to others in the body as well. I have been sharing this with everyone I know and they have all agreed with it and are excited to see this restoration take place.

—M.R., California

To be blunt, I am totally disillusioned with the church as a whole.... Let me say here that I am not a "nut." I work full time for a very well known Christian ministry, I travel on weekends and sing and teach and preach, I am the founder and president of [a Texas-based ministry] .... My heart, however, is breaking when I see the multitudes of people in our churches who have nothing to do and don't even have a real, vital relationship with Jesus Christ. I am constantly meeting people who have become disillusioned, have been hurt, have been shut out, and even ostracized simply because they know there is something more than what we have had in the church.

—T.S., Texas

We had gone from about 60 to 15—with the children making up over half. When I told my pastor that this [minibook] is what we needed, he got angry. It wasn't received until he was confiding in me that he was going to send out résumés, and I said, "Why not try a service that lets the Holy Spirit lead totally since there's nothing to lose?" So we went ahead, and by Easter Sunday we had 50 people.... This meeting way is true because it acknowledges the fulness of Him as He dwells within His people.

—L.A., New York

I am amazed to see that the three items of your agenda are the same three goals over which I have been wrestling with our God. As a minister of the Gospel, I just despise being an entertainer.

—L.H., Pennsylvania

Please, please, please send the booklet. I am so weary of the spectatorism that our culture promotes, and the damage that it does to our churches when professing Christian people carry it with them into our church gatherings

—Pastor J.D., New York

Bull's eye!! Are you ever right on target in your analysis AND with your Rx. I am already re-adjusting my [pastoral] style and strategy.... I—along with the entire Christian community here in the states—owe you a debt of gratitude. You've done the church a favor. Few these days have the courage to tell the rest of us that the "emperor has no clothes on." But how desperately we need to hear and face these unpleasant realities.... It's as if the church is in the Recovery Room, and God has placed the likes of you (& others) there to slap our faces til we awaken from this drunken stupor.... If enough of us rise up and say "enough!" then things will change.   —W.G., North Carolina

My wife and I dropped out of church in despair, distrust, and disgust. We are happier meeting with one other couple than one thousand in the traditional setting. I am leading now, and finally, after 30 years of blah-blah, I am growing. Men must be men to be anything of use.... My wife and I are pediatricians. You would not go to a physician who only read and schooled, but never treated a single case. Yet that is exactly what traditional church does: all teaching—no internship, no residency, nada!... Don't forget about us little guys. Keep on writing! **YES!**
                                    —Dr. & Dr. M.T., Missouri

I really don't have words to express my profound agreement with your article/advertisement. I literally broke into tears after reading it.   —T.K., Michigan

Despite the snake-oil-pusher's tone of your ad, you have hit a chord in this clergyperson. I know you're right about unscriptural and unspiritual worship, and ministers for decades have known it (including Søren Kierkegaard, whose "God is the audience" image you quoted).   —K.K., New York

Our church had struggled for 6 years with a handful of people. Since June we have grown to 150 people and are outgrowing our facilities by leaps and bounds. So please know that God is speaking your message that ministry must be restored to the people.
                                    —Pastor J.N., South Carolina

8
The Fast Track:
The Best Way to Change

by Gene Edwards

How can you turn the meetings of your church into open meetings? That is what this chapter is about: how to make open meetings practical.

Perhaps the best way I can approach this chapter is to put myself
back into the pastorate and ask myself, "What would I do if I were a
pastor and wanted to open the meetings?" This chapter, then, is for
pastors.

First of all, I would make sure that I had the backing and understanding of the people in my congregation.

Second, I would speak on the subject of open meetings for an extended period of time, and thereby allow my people to come to understand that we are on the threshold of a breath taking, unprecedented
change in our church.

I would let everyone in on the practical details. That is, I would
share with them everything mentioned in this chapter.

Now, where can you get some resources to aid you in speaking on
the open church? An open church is, after all, an idea that is new to
most ministers. Let me recommend a few books to you which will
help you in this area.[27]

---

27. The only book that really covers the do's and don'ts of Christian meetings is
How to Meet (available November, 1992). A much briefer treatment is the booklet,
There's a New Church Coming, intended as a hand-out or mail-out for churches just
starting the changeover. *Revolution* and *Going to Church in the First Century* are
also described in the bibliography. All are available through The SeedSowers.

Speak on the subject for several weeks before and during the time you begin implementing the practical steps.

Messages are not magic. Speaking on this subject will not produce open meetings. Which brings us to a very vital point!

Burn this into your mind: Your people *do not* know how to function; they have not even the foggiest notion. Miss that point, and you will miss having an open church. Your people need help, very practical help, and lots of it. Just preaching on the subject will produce nothing.

For your people to make the transition from being "sitters and listeners" to "sharers and participators" takes more than just asking your people to volunteer to get involved. There is a preparation period and a transition period that is needed. Fortunately, there *is* a way for you to give your people practical help, and they will respond to it! Expect the outcome to be beautiful and, unequivocally, one of the greatest high points of a believer's life and the life of your church.

Step 1

Have your people meet in homes one night a week for a period of five weeks *before* that first open meeting in the church building.

They must meet in homes in an informal situation for a good length of time before an open meeting in the church building. There is *no* substitute for this. Neglect this, and give up the whole idea. Do it, and you can have *great expectations.*

Next, and this is a hard one: *There must be no appointed leader in these home meetings.* What goes on inside those home meetings must *not* be organized. NO designated leaders. None! And only the barest instruction of what to do in those home meetings. *Minimum* instruction. This is an absolute essential. Forfeit this, and you greatly reduce informality and spontaneity in meetings held in the church building for months to come. Repeat: Your people do *not* know how to function, and these home meetings are as necessary as air is to life if your people are to move in the direction of whole-hearted participation in meetings.

Needed: Living Rooms

Volunteers will be needed to offer the living rooms of their homes for the meetings.

How would I go about enlisting my people in such a simple matter? I would use the announcement to signal to my people what I mean by *informality*. I would *not* set up a committee to get these volunteers, nor would I do any of those other things which churches have the bad habit of doing. Rather, I would call for volunteers right there in the Sunday morning service, and make it fun in so doing.

To wit: "Two weeks from now, we begin. Hal and Sandy have volunteered their home for Thursday night. Hal, what's your address? All right, exactly where *is* that? Near the what? Okay, we need eight volunteers who live in that area to meet in Hal and Sandy's home every Thursday for five weeks. Before you volunteer, remember you already know what you're getting into. *'If you show up, you speak up!'* Hal, write down their names. After the meeting, Hal, stay where you are. These eight people will come to you and give you their phone numbers, and you give them yours."[28]

"But doing it this way could take up almost the whole hour, and I'd be left with ten minutes for my sermon."

Great! That will *really* impress your people as to how important this is. You now have, say, twenty groups with about ten adults in each group meeting every Thursday night for the next *five* weeks.[29]

That first meeting must be a *non-meeting*. Explain it this way: Just get together and eat a meal together.

Spend the evening getting to know one another and sharing your hearts. Nothing else. What will you do at this first meeting? Just sit around and talk. Get to know one another a little. That is all.

Tell them to return thanks for the meal *after* the meal is over, just to avoid getting started on a religious or ritualistic note!

Make sure the first meeting comes with virtually *no* instructions.

"Be willing to prepare meals and do a little cleanup. Begin about 6:30. Quit when you are all ready to go home."

This is probably not the way you usually "organize" something,

---

28. So you have 3,000 people in your Sunday morning meeting and doing this at that time would take hours? All right, try the evening meeting. First, have homes selected before the Sunday meeting. Then, on Sunday evening have all the different "hosts" stand around the outer ring of the pews. Each host couple can speak out and identify exactly where their home is located. Now have the people who plan to meet in those homes leave their seats and go stand with the couple whose home is nearest to where they live. Stick with this until you have your two or three hundred groups of 10 to 12. Have them meet and exchange addresses.

29. Be sure to have some home meetings scheduled for Tuesday evening for people who can't get to a Thursday evening meeting. You may even have to schedule one or two Monday evening and Saturday evening meetings.

but you're putting a new hallmark on the way you are relating to the Lord's people.

Getting Started at Home

Now, let us talk about what happens at those five meetings. Meet and eat. Eat around the table or sit around the living room using TV trays or whatever. No ties! No dress-up. When dinner is over, clean up the mess. (Men included). Move to the living room. There in the living room everyone gives his or her name, telling a little bit about what they do and furnishing just enough information for clear identification.

What will that first meeting be like? Who knows! Just have it.

Will there be problems? Probably not. Not at the first meeting. But be open with your people about one *sure* long-range problem. Tell them to note the folks who are shy and those who are extroverts. Or, to put it another way, those who don't talk enough and those who talk too much.

In a group of ten, there should be at least one or two Christians who fall into either category. Tell your people this.

"Joan doesn't talk much, and you can't get Evelyn to stop. Joe is downright reclusive, and Jim is from Yarnsville, Texas! Some of you never talk, others of you inhale in the middle of your sentences so no one can interrrupt you at the end of your sentences."

Explain to your people that this is going to happen and that it is natural. This is the way it is *all over the world.* Ten people get together informally, some talk too much, some hardly at all.

"It is all right to be shy and all right to be outgoing. It is just that we will need, as the weeks unfold, for you two kinds of people — on the opposite ends of the spectrum — to move a little toward the middle. *Both* of you."

Trust your people. They will understand. They *will* respond!

Give them no more instruction than that! Tell them they are on their own!

Repeat: designate *no* leader for these meetings. None! If there is no leader present, your people will let their guard down. They *are* going to start talking to one another. They will get to know one another and begin to like one another. And they are going to love it!!

What of the four weeks after that first meeting?

Get together. Eat. Clean up the mess. Adjourn to the living room and...each week, *two* people present are to tell the story of their conversion and a little bit of their Christian life. That's it.

Yes, perhaps there could be a little singing and a little praying, but it is not obligatory. Learning to be together and sharing informally is *all* that is expected, and even these simple matters *may* take a little time. On the other hand, your people may take to these gatherings like a Sahara duck who just spotted H_2O for the first time.

This is not a time to get off on praying for one another's nosebleeds and hangnails, or chatting about baseball! If there is prayer, stay away from "prayer requests." Let any prayer be an expression of love and appreciation to the Lord.

That constitutes the next four weeks.

By the end of five weeks, everyone will, perhaps unconsciously, be loosened up, speaking with one another, and sharing. There is even a good chance the Lord's people will be caring for one another's needs (but hardly noticing that they are)!

Of course, they may also have learned how to sit around and sing a cappella! Singing in a living room! Singing that first began awful and has come all the way up to *fair*. (But whether awful or wonderful, God's people will have enjoyed their simple singing and simple prayers, and they will be amazed anything this simple and undirected could be so delicious!

Is that all? Is it that simple? Yes. All you need now is to make sure everyone knows the date of that *first* open meeting when the entire ecclesia is together in one place.

Step 2: The First Open Meeting

For this first rattle-out-of-the-box meeting, I recommend you choose a Sunday night.

And if you don't have a Sunday night church service? I recommend you call a special one for this particular meeting. Why Sunday night? Because *all* of you need to sneak up on Sunday morning. People who are perfectly normal the rest of the week, get downright strange on Sunday morning. Folks are *afraid* of Sunday morning when it comes to functioning.

Now, dear brother, I implore you: Leave your tie and suit at home on this auspicious occasion. And ask the rest of the men to do likewise, and ask the women not to dress up fancy!

Next: When the meeting begins, I implore you *not* to stand in the front of the auditorium or in the pulpit. Either get lost somewhere in the pews, or, if you must, go to the middle of the auditorium, and do any speaking from there.[30]

If you have the courage, go even further: state the purpose of the meeting and then *leave the room.* (Go bowling! Take a nap! Let your wife tell you what happened in the meeting after she gets home!)

If you really want to be bold, as you walk out, take the minister of music, the minister of education, the pianist, the organist and all other perceived leaders out of the building with you.

And if you want to live out on the edge of good sense, here is *the money-back guaranteed best way of all.* Announce that the meeting will begin in *this* unique way:

"The Sunday evening gathering is at 7 p.m.. The doors of the auditorium will be closed when you arrive. We will all gather out in front of the auditorium. We will gather outside, we will sing together out there for awhile, packed in as close to one another as possible. Then the doors will open. When they do, 'all us great church leaders' will go off to Denny's for dinner. All of us! We will *not* be hiding in the building somewhere, nor will we have a spy present with a recording device. The meeting is utterly open. Once you walk through that door, you are on your own!"

Because this is the first time for anyone to do this, and those first crucial minutes are so important, instruct each group to agree upon one person in their group to be the first to share in the meeting: "We have twenty groups. One person in each group has been chosen to share first for his or her group. If you know you have something to share, stand up and await your turn."

A practice of quiet waiting can truly help your people meet. If two or three stand at once to say something, all should remain standing. Also, if someone is in the midst of sharing and the Lord moves in another's heart to share, he should just quietly stand up and wait his "turn in line" to speak.

This will be a real encouragement to everyone. They'll know that someone else is about to share. And when someone is halfway through, and what he says touches three other hearts, *they* should stand and wait their turns to deliver their messages or prayers or songs. At that point, *everyone* will be excited. "Three whole people have something they're itching to say! Wow!"

Please note: When you stand, it **doesn't** mean, "I wish you'd hurry

---

30. This applies to the first meeting only. After that, you should try not to lead the meeting.

up and finish so I can say my piece." Contrariwise, it means, "Please take your time. I'm so moved by what you're saying that I'd like to tack a complementary thought onto yours when you're done."

Moreover, queuing joins each person's contribution with the others', creating a new unity.

With those instructions...vanish. Trust your **God and trust** your people. They will thank you for it!!

That meeting may be all sharing, no singing, no prayer. That is all right. Later remind them that in future meetings, songs can be interspersed between testimonies and that Scripture can be interspersed with teaching and worship, and prayer can be interspersed between anything!

Other Instructions

Share the following with your people!

No one should speak for over three to five minutes.

When you share, it is all right to cry, but if you start taking the whole meeting to cry, someone who loves you very dearly should come over, put their arm around you and help you finish. If that doesn't do it, give up trying, graciously sit down and try again *next* week.

When you share, say nothing that could be construed as a criticism of another person. And remember, this is not a forum to extract revenge on someone you don't like. Keep it positive.

This one may surprise you. I would like to suggest the piano and the organ not be used in an open meeting. (Ditto for the guitar.) Using them puts the focus on the person with the musical intrument rather than the singing, and it also clogs up the flow of the meeting. *After a few meetings of practice, everyone will be amazed at how beautiful the singing has become!*

The first time everyone gathers for a meeting in the church building, you *may* still want to break your people up into several groups, meeting in different parts of the building. One in the auditorium, one in the fellowship hall, one in a large Sunday school assembly room, etc. (Reason: If your church is quite large, you may wish to "sneak up" on the whole-church meeting gradually.)

If you are fortunate enough to have a church building that has folding chairs that can be moved around, I am going to recommend that you consider arranging your chairs in a very specific way. Here, in my experience, is the best way, to arrange chairs. It causes everyone to be facing everyone else:

   You will notice that there is a center, but you, the minister, should
not be sitting in that center. (Go to your office and read a good book.
Or if you must, slip out of the room for fifteen minutes and then sneak
back in as unnoticed as possible. Or just go home and fix that leak
in the kitchen sink!)
   If you don't particularly take a shine to this *most perfect* way of
arranging chairs, here are two more possiblities:

   The first way is the best. If you don't agree, try some other way.
Then, when the open meeting has taken root, come back to this arrangement and see if it doesn't work best.
   Never, repeat, *never* put the chairs in a circle. A circle may seem
like an open, egalitarian idea; but it absolutely *does not work!* Why?
I suppose because it's just *too* open and intimidating. There's nothing to hide behind!
   If you have pews, *you have my deepest sympathy!* You need to
give very special attention to this problem, and it *is* a problem. Before that first meeting even begins, encourage this:
   "Those of you who sit in the front half of the auditorium...when
you stand to share, turn and face the folks behind you. Speak to
everyone.
   "Those seated in the front seats also need to turn a bit in their pews

in order to be able to see the other half of the gathering."

Next, and chisel this in stone: *There must not be a moderator.* If there is a moderator, everyone will speak directly to that person. That will ruin the whole meeting.

Perhaps for the first few meetings, tell your people they can pick out one person to look at while they are talking; just don't pick the pastor! (After a few weeks, they will have forgotten they ever needed this crutch. Your people will get so used to this kind of meeting it will amaze you.)[31]

There are those in every gathering of God's people who cannot project their voices. They simply cannot be heard. I do not know how to solve this problem. Write to me if *you* do!

I would suggest that everyone involved in this entire adventure be armed with a songsheet of 20 to 50 very simple, very beautiful songs and hymns. They should first use them in the home meetings. Everyone should then bring the songsheets to those first church-wide meetings.

Now, what about singing? Some of your people ... no, all of your people will want to announce songs *this* way: "May we sing Number 21?"

Don't let this happen.

The bolder ones will say it this way: "NUMBER 21!"

---

31. What is "this kind of meeting"? An open one, to be sure. But more than that, it is a *leaderless* meeting in human terms. In actuality, the meeting is being led by *Christ himself,* through the Holy Spirit.

But even on a human plane, it is not a leaderSHIPless meeting; the leaders, the elders, and the more sensitive of the brothers all provide active (not hierarchical) leadership by all they share and do.

In high contrast, Ray Stedman advises in absolute terms in Chapter 13 that his type of open, body-life meeting *requires* that you have a leader—and a strong one, at that! The apparent disagreement by two men with long experience fades away when you consider the nature of the two kinds of open meetings and their intended outcome:

Stedman is talking about sharing-type meetings where worship seldom becomes the main focus. These meetings are large affairs with quite a few casual visitors who are uninformed on even the basics of sharing and body life. Though they frequently produce results that are advanced indeed, their *dynamics* are usually pretty ordinary. Everyone present is perfectly free to share, but a degree of emcee control is expected.

Edwards is talking about comprehensive meetings designed to lift all the participants to a new level of involvement in leadership, worship, and corporate response to the *Spirit's* leading. In that setting, an emcee's presence would simply annihilate an individual's hesitant, stumbling efforts to grow in leadership. —J.R.

Don't let this happen, either.

Show your people how to announce a song. *(This single instruction will revolutionize your meetings!)* "When you want to sing a certain song, do not ask everyone's permission! And do not announce the number. Just *begin singing!* We will join you!"

Some will say, "I can't start a song." No problem. Poke your neighbor, point to the song, and say, "Start this song." (Neighbor, start the song!)

After the song is started and well on its way, for the sake of visitors, someone should then announce, loud and clear, "Number 21!" Your visitors, now dumfounded at such an incredible flowing of the meeting, will find Number 21 and join in. Explain to your people that as soon as someone begins singing, *everyone* should join in, announce the number *after* the song starts.

Your people should *never* wait until everybody rattles their songsheets and looks through the sheets until they find Number 21. "Just start singing. Later you can find your songsheet, and find Number 21."

After a few weeks, your people will have made this a part of their lives. Someone stands and shares. As soon as he sits down, someone else stands to take his place. After some significant testimony, someone will start an appropriate song... *without* announcing the number. All this takes a little time to learn, but it comes if you will hold the course week after week. Encourage your people. They will work with you. They want this. It is innate to our species to want this. It will come, and when it comes, it will be beautiful.

That should do it, but let us take one more look at the "permanent problem" of open meetings.

Operation O-F-F

You need to let your people know ahead of time that, "There are some among us who simply talk too long. And some who talk too little." This fact will become evident to everyone during those five home meetings.

What can be done? The first is simply to tell your people to expect this. That is half the solution right there.

Second, I suggest you do the following in the home meetings, and tell your people ahead of time that this will be done: Have the saints in the home meetings designate a sister—not a brother—to call time on the *o*ver *f*unctioning *f*ellows! She will say to the *o*ver *functioning fellow:* "Joe, about one more minute." It works. (This, of course, is called "Operation OFF.")

I have a friend who actually employs a kitchen timer in his meetings! The bell sounds after three to five minutes. I haven't done this, but I think it may be a good idea. The only thing I would add is that I would let all my people know that once the bell has sounded, they have one more minute in order to conclude.

This matter of the over-talker does not have to be handled as though it were a big problem, especially if you introduce it long before even the home meetings. *I have never seen offense taken when handled this way.*

Do keep in mind that, like the poor, the over-functioner will always be with us. So here is one more card to play: the magpie contest.

I have been in open meetings in which I have asked everyone in the room to write down the names of the people who don't function enough and of those who over function. For the name that wins the most votes for the least functioning person, we agree ahead of time, that whoever he/she is, that person will be the first one to share at the *next* meeting. And the winner(s) of the *magpie* contest will share only *once* in the next meeting! (Not ten times like they did in the *last* meeting.) And, they will be *timed,* and limited to five minutes. Again, approached in this way, I have never seen anyone offended. There is nothing that will take the place of facing a problem before it arises, and then facing it again with sterling good humor. Later, you will see your people, in home meetings, inventing their own ways to handle this ever-with-us problem.

Closing the Meeting

There should be someone in all gatherings (not someone considered to be a leader, but just an ordinary peasant) who is designated to end the meeting. Remember, there is no form here, so there is no set ritual and no set time that ends a meeting. Now, if the end has been announced, but someone feels the meeting should continue, then go along with them, at least for a few more minutes. Some of the best meetings I will ever be in came after someone declared, "This meeting is over," and someone else said, "I'd like to share just a word before we go."

One Special Meeting

A meeting will come one day that should not be ended. If it lasts until midnight, let it last until midnight. It may happen in the homes or in the building, but it *will* happen. On that day, give the Holy Spirit His right to move among God's people. You will be very, very glad you didn't watch your watch.

In this chapter, I've assumed your church is fairly united on these matters. If this is not the case, you may need some other ways to proceed. In the four chapters ahead, Jim Rutz describes the best alternatives.

9
The Middle of the Road Track: Top Down

Here's another approach. And it's easy.

Start with the coaches instead of the players. Have them call the opening plays from the sidelines. After that, let the players improvise on their own.

Work from the top down, allowing the existing leadership to launch the changes. Rather than making the effort to retrain all the players *before* the kickoff, have the head coach toss them the ball and then tell them how to run with it.

In this game plan, rather than turning your entire service into a time of open worship, sharing, and ministry, the leaders will probably want to designate a certain limited period or "time out" for open worship and another for open sharing.

The top-down approach gives the leaders more control. That's the best *and* worst thing about it! (Pastoral proctorship is a killer. In an open meeting, freedom and surveillance can't coexist.)

Top-down is your best option when:

- The coaches are quick to catch on to the new game, but the players aren't.
- The coaches decide that the players aren't in shape for the new season yet.
- The coaches are nervous about the new game rules and begin to perspire heavily at the thought of truly letting go of the ball.
- The *players* are nervous about the new game rules and begin murmuring about not suiting up for the opening game.
- Both the players and the coaches are tired of playing the old game, but they don't understand the new one.
- The players are a grab bag of foot-draggers and sheep. They act

like the local chapter of Zombies For Jesus.

As you can see, top-down is Plan B. It may not be the fastest or *most solid* way to produce a fully open team. It may be a bit of a cop-out. But when you foresee that Plan A just isn't an option for some reason, top-down is B-OK. It will work just fine.

Once you find that Gene Edwards' Plan A is out, here is a typical game plan for the middle-of-the-road, top-down approach...

1. **Pray.** Ask God for a good, clear vision of what He wants your church to look and act like two years from now.

2. **Memorize** Hebrews 10:37-39:

"For yet a little while—so little—and the Coming One shall come, and shall not tarry; but My righteous one shall live by faith, and if he shrinks back, My soul has no pleasure in him. Surely we are not going to be men who cower back to eternal misery..." [blended translation]

3. **Make a list** of all the good things that would happen in your church if it opened up. (You may want to skim over Part I again to refresh your memory.)

Then study your list to identify the biggest benefits (as you see them). Get them firmly set in your mind so you can discuss them with your friends without using notes.

Do a lot of creative thinking. Construct a vision of what your church might be like with an open format. Plug that vision into your prayers.

4. In most cases, I suppose, you'll want to **have a good talk** with one or two of your friends in the church. Lend them this book or get them to buy a copy. Or failing that, get some copies of the super-cheap, super-condensed version, *The Rebirth of the Church*[32], and give them one.

Then after they've read the material, have another good talk. *Perhaps you could have a "dream session," discussing the benefits of opening your church.* I'd also suggest praying with each one.

(Two friends are probably about enough. If you talk with ten or fifteen before you approach the pastor and elders, it starts to look like you're trying to gang up on them—and you probably are! *Don't!*)

---

32. Full title: *The Exciting Fellowship of Long Ago, Lost for 1700 Years, Is Coming Back. Get Ready for The Rebirth of the Church.* You may obtain a packet of ten copies from The SeedSowers. You can use the order card in the back of this book. If the order card is missing, the address is P.O. Box 3368, Auburn, Maine 04212, and the price for ten is ten dollars postpaid. This 36-page booklet comprises mainly Part I of *The Open Church.*

5. **Talk with your pastor, elders, or diaconate.** You might bring along a friend or two for moral support. I'd suggest that you...
   a. Be truly enthusiastic, but not nutty.
   b. Tell them concisely what "open church" means.
   c. Make a positive presentation of all the *benefits* of opening the church.
   d. Tell them exactly what you'd like them to do. Outline briefly a possible series of concrete steps and actions they could take to open the church from the top down. For example:
      (1) Read this book, then seek the mind of the Lord about implementing it.
      (2) Prepare the congregation for open worship, sharing, and ministry with a series of two or three sermons or lessons in Sunday School classes.
      (3) Begin with a period of open worship OR sharing, whichever they think will be the easiest and most foolproof to start with.
      (4) When the church starts responding well, diversify into the second area. Then into open ministry—if that hasn't started by itself in the open sharing time.
   e. In conclusion, emphasize that this is not a matter of taste or tradition, but God's pattern as seen in Scripture. And recap the main benefits tactfully.
6. Remember to faithfully **pray for them.**
7. During the weeks the pastor is giving his preparatory sermons, **talk to as many in the church as you can** about the benefits of opening the church, recognizing the priesthood of every believer, and launching a whole new and exciting way of "doing church."

Always stress the spiritual growth, the freedom, and the joy of being a true body. Try *not* to criticize the current structure. (If people read this book or *The Rebirth of the Church*, that will provide more than enough unsolicited criticism!)

And *puh-leeze* be sure to present this as a simplifying process, not a complicating one!

10
The Chicken Track: Slow and Safe

On to Plan C.

What if everyone admires your flag, but no one will salute it? What if they all agree that the open church is orthodox as a dollar bill, but nobody has the nerve to reach out his hand and take it?

If your officers are too hesitant to lead the charge and the troops are too nervous to follow, then what does a bright, persistent person like you do? Why, you simply move right ahead—albeit more slowly.

You don't squawk like a turkey or make a fuss. If your Christian flock is a flock of chickens, you'd better learn to lay eggs with the best of them! As St. Paul said, "I have become all things to all chickens..."

The Chicken Track is simply a variant of Plan B. In fact, you'll want to take exactly the same steps to get started, right up through step five, your presentation to the board.

Here is the variation. If they *don't* want to move ahead to restore your lost freedoms, then you shift gears, slip deftly into your three-piece chicken suit, and say something like this:

I understand 100%. You like several of the remarkable benefits we'd get with an open church, but you'd rather take a longer look at it first. That makes sense. You're concerned that we might encounter some problems down the line, and you want to be prepared for them. You also wish to make sure that the congregation is really behind this, so you want them to be involved and committed before you move ahead. I think that's a wise motivation.

So in order to proceed carefully without running the risk of passing up an opportunity that I feel is scriptural and from the Lord, may I make four small suggestions that I think will fit into your priorities at this point? *[Wait politely for their assent.]*

OK, first, we could use some input on the subject from some more of the best minds in the congregation. A committee of good, clear thinkers could read *The Open Church*, investigate the whole matter, and report back to us in two months with a recommendation on how to proceed, if at all.

Second, it would be exciting to invite in a speaker or consulting team from Open Church Ministries. Or even have them put on a seminar here that we could jointly sponsor with other churches.

Third, you on the board could review one book each and compare notes a month from now. I know the names of the best books on the subject of open churches.[33] Of course, you'll also probably want to look at *The Open Church*. You'll find it's fun to read.

Fourth, I'd be happy to provide everyone in the congregation with a copy of *The Rebirth of the Church*, a very condensed version of *The Open Church*. I guarantee it will convince a lot of the members and smooth the way toward some initial trial programs.

I really believe this will do more to strengthen our members and enlarge our church than anything else we'll ever see in our lifetime. And my four-point plan allows us to be as cautious as possible in looking at it.

I see the open church movement as something that will grow rapidly all across the country, bringing a lot of benefits to the little guys like me who really need and want to get into the heart of God's work. I feel it's only fair to our members to give them a chance to learn about it. And who knows? Maybe they'll all be excited and want to dive right in! In that case, you wouldn't want to hold them back, would you?

Of course, that isn't *exactly* what you'll say to the board, but it should give you some thoughts to go on.

Whatever you say, keep it positive and simple. Emphasize what the church will gain rather than what it's lacking now. And make

---

33. See the annotated bibliography on page 185.

sure they get a feel for how this will strengthen both the church and each individual member.

As the weeks go on, you'll find the Holy Spirit will use all the reading, study, and discussion throughout the church to create an unstoppable firestorm for change.

11
The Mission Track:
Starting Somewhere Else

And now we slog onward to Plan D, grimly humming the melody line from "Still will we trust, though earth seem dark and dreary."

Just kidding, of course. By this point in your Christian life, I hope you've seen enough of the power and sovereignty of God to realize that sometimes our "last resort" plans are His first resort. Often, your last ditch effort will turn out to be far superior to the smooth-looking Plan A you had your heart set on.

So also here. *If the God-appointed leaders of your church will not even agree to study and pray about having an open church, rejoice!* What comes next in your life may be the most breathtaking event of all: an opportunity for you to pioneer a whole fresh, new matrix of fellowship.[34]

If you pray and meditate and proceed in a godly fashion to approach your pastor, elders, or diaconate, and they still won't allow any changes in the Sunday worship service—or agree to back up laymen who receive ministry gifts/assignments directly from God—then you are looking at Plan D: starting somewhere other than the Sunday morning service.

You will have two alternatives:
1. Start an open fellowship as part of your present church.
2. Start an open fellowship as a mission/daughter church.

Let's take #1 first.

---

34. Sorry, there's no real synonym for "matrix." It means here a source, well-spring, hotbed, nucleus, breeding place, or womb. It's a network of friendships that generates body life.

Welcome to the *Minichurch*, the Stepchild of the '80s

Thirty per cent. That's a safe bet.

If I were a betting man, I'd wager that at least three out of ten evangelical Christians you tell about the open church will agree with you right off the bat—*instinctively*.

Everything about open worship, sharing, and ministry just hits many believers right, and they *feel* it's right in their hearts even before they have a clear idea of what you're talking about.

And after you do some explaining and reasoning, that 30% can grow in time to 60% or 70%. After all, the open church is God's idea, and the indwelling Holy Spirit soon confirms to the godly mind that, yes, this seems right and good and desirable ... even while the intellect (the loyal opposition) is dutifully scraping up questions and objections.

What I'm saying is that Christians sensitive to the intent of the Holy Spirit have a natural desire for an open church *even if they can't verbalize it*. That explains the modest proliferation of mini-churches in the 1980s.

Now, a mini-church is not a congregation of mini-Christians. A mini-church is a house church **within** an institutional church. A subgroup or division. And they tend to be rather open.

During the '80s, thousands of North American churches sprouted mini-churches because of the felt need to have something like an open church. Lively parishioners in a wide variety of churches began meeting weekly in homes on Sunday nights, Tuesday nights, etc., sharing and caring, giving and receiving, praying and doing all manner of good stuff they couldn't do Sunday morning.

I expect them to continue and prosper in the '90s even though most are still more closed than they might be. Some of their leaders have only a shadowy idea of what a Spirit-led, open meeting looks like, and that's a real handicap. But even so, people have found mini-churches to be a far superior source of life-changing interaction. If you're interested in personal and community growth, you want an open church. And a mini-church usually has enough open worship, sharing, and ministry to make a closed, traditional church look bleak and sterile in comparison.

I talk to a fair number of pastors, telling them about the open church. Often their response is a quick, "Oh, we do all that!"

Now, I know they're not trying to lie to me. But I also know that it's usually just not true. Their church is probably as traditional as the vault in a bank, and just as closed. So I eagerly reply, "Zat*so!*" and stare them in the eye and wait.

In most cases, they continue with the clarification, "Yeah, we have mini-churches that meet during the week in homes, and they all...etc., etc."

"Aha!" I chortle to myself, "Another Plan D church!"

Three-Fourths of a Loaf Is Better Than None At All

I adore mini-churches. Wish we had a million of 'em. They're putting forth a great effort, and they give people *much* of what they would get in a self-governing, self-perpetuating open church.

But the reality is that they're still captive to a closed church. They're a bright and glorious band-aid on a horrible, gaping hole in the institutional church. As such, they ironically perpetuate the closed church system by making up for many of its shortcomings! They virtually guarantee a permanent future for it, warts and all.

Moreover, their subsidiary position keeps a 600-pound lid on their scope, their growth possibilities, their gift development, their sense of responsibility, the authority of their leaders—factors that can power a young congregation to growth and maturity. For example:

- You'll rarely see a mini-church outgrowing its parent or sending out missionaries on its own or establishing autonomous daughter churches in other towns.
- You'll rarely see a wedding, funeral, or baptism conducted under the auspices of a mini-church; such functions are reserved for the professional staff of the *real* church, the parent church.
- You'll rarely see a mini-church:
  - developing pastors who are allowed to preach and officiate in the parent church
  - sponsoring teachers with a regional or national ministry
  - choosing delegates to attend the denomination's convention (and perhaps encourage the formation of more open fellowships).

In theory, mini-churches could grow and grow forever, becoming the tail that wags the dog.

In practice, they're like a perpetual teenager who's never allowed to leave home and set up house on his own. They become a permanent *play*-church. You might diagram their position like this:

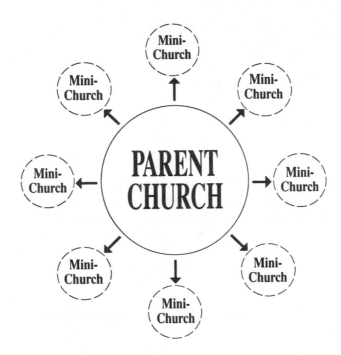

That's not to say they're inferior to their parent churches. Over-all, I think they're superior. In mini-churches you'll find love shared, souls saved, disciples built, truth discovered, darkness dispelled, and lives healed more often than in their institutional parents.

But mini-churches aren't the solution to the problem, just the best way I know of helping us *live with it.* Permanently!

The Alternative Service: Seven-Eighths of a Loaf

Back around 1969, I started five "encounter groups" under the wary auspices of the singles ministry at the famed Hollywood Presbyterian Church in L.A. Great fun! (No rules.) Sitting on the floor in a circle in somebody's apartment was the closest thing to an open church that my tiny brain could envision at the time.

It was at the height of the wonderful "Jesus people" movement, and HollyPres was at the center of the action, as usual. Born-again hippies and flower children were crawling in the windows, figuratively, and the staid, upscale church didn't quite know what to do with them.

One thing was certain: The genteel elements that ran the joint had sharply limited enthusiasm for Christian togetherness when it came to rubbing elbows with a horde of highly unPresbyterian Woodstock dropouts and Jesus freaks.

As there seemed to be no way to sanitize and upgrade them to a sufficiently lofty socio-sartorial level, the leadership soon fastened upon the obvious solution: apartheid.

Yes sir, they decided to give the sandaled set their very own **Alternative Worship Service.** One proviso, however: The thing would have to start early enough so that the early arrivers for the (*ahem*) *regular* first service at 9:30 a.m. wouldn't have to mingle with the hairy/unwashed stragglers leaving the Alternative Service.

As I remember, after some negotiation, the leadership issued a final offer, "You guys do whatever you want, but it has to start *before 8:20.*"

Now, if you've ever had kids, you know what the response was. The eager young crowd instantly proclaimed the inauguration of **The 8:19 Service.** And thus it was called till the day it died.

Like the Jesus people movement itself, it didn't last forever, but it served as a fine model for other churches dealing desperately with diversity. Since those heady days, numerous other congregations have tried all sorts of alternative services for all sorts of reasons—with all sorts of results.

Here and there they have worked, and continue to this day to give bored/antsy/despairing believers a way to escape the restrictions and rituals of their church without actually leaving (which should always be the *last* resort). Also, a number of mainline denominational churches have been touched by the charismatic movement, and in response have begun an alternative service as a way to accommodate their new diversity (read: avoid a church split).

In most cases, launching an alternative service—with its own nucleus of influence—will be a more promising avenue for you than the mini-church route. That's because you'll have more perceived legitimacy, a bigger arena, and far better chances of seeing the rest of the church wander in to test the waters. As you read chapter 13 on the success story of Peninsula Bible Church, you'll see a shining example of an alternative service that spread to every nook of the church.

On the negative side, you'll still have *some* of the limitations of both the institutional and mini-church. Also, having an alternative service makes you very visible, so expect closer scrutiny from the elders and pastor—which could mean less freedom to experiment.

But if you're offered the chance for an alternative service, take it. At the start, you may feel as unwanted as those outcast proto-hippies who were banished to the Calvinist limbo of the 8:19 hour. That's all right. Time will be on your side. And so will God.

Starting a Mission/Daughter Church: A Whole Nother Ball Game

This isn't putting a band-aid on your arm. This is growing a whole new arm.

It's not the tactical equivalent of an end run in football. It's launching a whole new league.

If, in the sovereignty and timing of God, your church board flat-out refuses to allow a restoration of the three freedoms: open worship, open sharing, and open ministry ... refuses to allow an alternative service ... and even refuses to allow an open mini-church within their structure ... you still have one excellent option left: forming a whole new church—an open church—as a mission project or daughter church.

Some church boards simply don't want any heat around their doors. But often they'll become quite co-operative if they can keep the controversy at arm's length. So if you have prayed and made a decent presentation to them (and perhaps have a few respected, level-headed members in your corner), you may be surprised to see them make an about-face and offer their whole-hearted support to help you start a brand new, open church as a spin-off project.

If that happens, take another look at Chapter Eight (on the fast track). You'll be able to apply most of its suggestions to help your new fellowship get off on the right foot.

Tips on Launching a Mission/Daughter Church

Look both inside and outside your church for prospective members, but don't set your mind on starting with big numbers. Take whom God sends you, prepare them as well as you can for your initial meetings, and move ahead joyfully, without delay.

But in your heart, think in pictures of what it will look like in five or ten years. Envision your small start-up group as a future Peninsula Bible Church or Phoenix First Assembly. Or think of it as phase one of an explosion of churches.

You might diagram a small family of autonomous, open churches something like this:

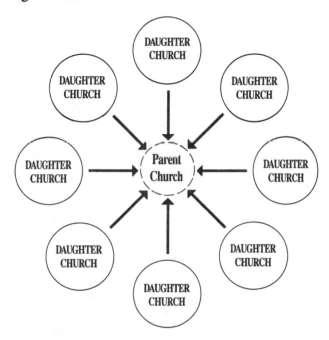

In such a pattern, the parent church might function mostly as a rallying point for special events or larger meetings from time to time.

Some suggested steps:

1. Gather up your address book, your church directory (if your board has approved of this), your Christmas card list—all your lists of friends and neighbors. Then ask God who could profit from being in a church where they were part of the action, not part of the scenery. Be prepared to start making lots of check marks!

2. After you've gone through your lists, select a specific set of names to begin with, perhaps ten, perhaps twenty. Pray some more, then talk to each one quietly but enthusiastically, emphasizing whatever aspects of the open church *you* find most appealing. Stress the *benefits*, not the theory. (Even after inflation, theories are a dollar a dozen.)

3. At the close of each initial conversation, suggest your friend read this book or the Open Church Ministries brochure, *The Rebirth of the Church* (and/or perhaps another book from the bibliography). The best procedure is to lend them a copy, as this allows you to re-

cycle it and save money *while committing your friend to reading it within an agreed time* (about a week is ideal for the book, 3-4 days for the brochure).[35] You'll need several copies.

Selling it works well, too. But don't just give it away. That can get expensive, and they may never read it.

4. Follow up punctually. Always ask, "How did you like it?" Then pray some more and check back from time to time; don't annoy, but persist.

5. Select a new batch of names from your lists and repeat the process until you reach a desirable number *and variety* of people to start meeting with. Whatever you do, don't just mail out 200 copies of the brochure and sit back to see what will happen; very little will!

6. If you've never led or spearheaded anything before, you may feel awkward. In fact, you may feel like a class B scrounger attempting to push your pet ideas on the world.

You have my permission to ignore these feelings! Remember the truth: You're on a mission to transform problem-plagued lives, save people from hell, help a suffering world, and bring delight to Him who sits on the rainbow-encircled throne.

The Worst Case Scenario

Suppose your board just says no to everything. Or even worse, hardly anyone in your church shows much enthusiasm for the idea of an open church. What do you do then?

You pray and wait and watch for an opening.

If you're really starved for meaningful worship, fellowship, and service, you'll eventually probably consider starting a new church without the active support and backing of your old church, or even changing to another church.[36] I can't advise you specifically on that without knowing you. But I can tell you that being a regular church-hopper is not God's plan for anyone.

A rolling stone gathers no moss, and it's a telling comment on our age that we now think it's *good* to gather no moss. Just a few years

---

35. I personally feel that your book expenses (Bibles, tracts, etc.) can be counted as part of your tithe or your offering if you divide your money into sacred and secular compartments. But that's just one opinion.

36. Whatever you do, *don't* start another denomination! The body of Christ is already splintered into too many denominations, and our lack of unity is a disgrace. Always make every effort to align yourself with an existing group of churches.

ago, everyone understood that a stone staying in one place would gather a charming coat of emerald moss, quite unlike a barren boulder bouncing around and headed—predictably—downhill.

Whatever you do, don't turn into another A.W. Pink. That famous Bible teacher once wrote, "If there are any 'churches' which are scriptural in their membership, in their maintenance of discipline, in their preaching, and in all that concerns their public services, we do not know where to find them. We have traveled completely around the world ... but there is no church known to us where we could hold membership." So he and his wife remained at home on Sundays for the last three decades of his life—the ultimate house church!

On the next page, for lack of a better place, I'll present to you a few paragraphs from Ralph Neighbour of Touch Outreach Ministries in Houston. I have given you several open-church options that can leave your church's organizational structure intact, which is usually counted as a plus. But many church leaders feel a need for new wineskins along with the new wine of openness, and that's where Touch can help.

Whereas this book avoids suggesting new structures, Dr. Neighbour's well-written, 400-page book, *Where Do We Go from Here?*, gives a very detailed, proven, practical structure to copy. It seems to be working like gangbusters; he informs me that he now has four men answering the phones full time, counseling ministers on how to switch to his model.

During the past 35 years, a new form of church life has spread across the earth. It is estimated that as many as 75 million people are participating in "cell churches." It is rooted in the New Testament church pattern described in Acts 2:42-46. Like the early church, the movement forms small cells, called "Basic Christian Communities," which move from house to house. They typically begin with six to eight persons, multiplying in a period of 6-9 months to fifteen. At this point, each cell multiplies and grows again to the size for reproduction.

Unlike house churches, such cells are intimately related to one another, like those in a human body. The cell leader's task is to equip every Christian for the work of the ministry. Mature believers become responsible for apprenticing new believers in the group. Edification, or "building-up," is seen as a major activity of their gatherings. One writer has said, "In our cell group, we become the agents of grace for one another. We recognize that each one of us is called to build up the rest. We don't just have a weekly cell meeting; we live together as Christ's body."

They cluster into groups of five, with each group having a volunteer worker to minister to the cell leaders. These clusters often combine to create "congregations" composed of about 250 people for "congregational" events, like half nights of prayer, and also assemble for larger "celebrations" that may gather thousands for a weekly time of praise and Bible teaching. However, the thing that makes a cell church unique is that there's nothing to "join" except the "Basic Christian Community."

Cell churches have no geographical parishes. The Ichthus Fellowship of London, for example, has cells in Cyprus, Turkey and other Middle East nations. The Youpogon Church and Mission in Abidjan, Ivory Coast, has cell groups in Haiti, Paris, and five other African nations. The Faith Community Baptist Church of Singapore, just five years old, has over 5,000 people meeting in cells there and is sending teams of its members to several other Southeast Asian nations. Thailand has seen more believers through the single ministry of the "Hope of Thailand" cell church than any other group that has ever worked in that country.

In America, the cell church movement is presently exploding. Several hundred congregations are now discarding the "busy work" within church buildings for the reality of cell group ministries. They realize programs based in buildings must be set aside to provide time for edification and "body life" evangelism in members' homes. It is one of the fastest growing church structures in the world today, and points to the potential that open church ministries can produce for Christians in this generation.

—Ralph Neighbour

12
The Radical Track: Dynamite

You probably won't like this chapter much.

That's why I've put it at the end of Part III. And kept it short.

Actually, it should have been the *first* chapter, but I was afraid that some grouchy readers (not you, those other guys) would have popped the whole thing in the dumper before you could say, "Jack Daniels!" or whatever it is one says in such cases.

The difficulty is, this solution to the closed-church problem is for purists only, the super-committed disciples and scholars who want to follow the example of the New Testament *ekklesia* like a shadow. (I use the scriptural "ekklesia" because to purists, the word "church" is an outrageous concept forced on us by King James, who for political reasons *ordered* his translators to use it rather than the more obvious "assembly" or "gathering.")

Frankly, my friend, if you're a true-blue primitivist in every detail, you're not going to want a church *building* or just one single pastor at the helm of things. And that's only the beginning of your objections to today's institutional church! *If you want to revert to the exact scriptural pattern, you'll have to dissolve the pastorate, dynamite the sanctuary, and do a whole long list of other things*—some of which will leave your friends shaking their heads about you. (There, I said it and I'm glad.)

In the days of Peter and Paul, Christian church buildings were unthought of. The first "church building" was two centuries in the future.

And pastors were common, yes, but the idea of putting one in charge of a Christian flock probably never even occurred to anyone. Apostles were numerous, and they did make short visits to establish churches and appoint leaders, but they always appointed a *group* of leaders—and called them **elders**, not pastors.

The U.S. Christians who are most scrupulous about following the New Testament pattern are, hands down, the house church crowd. Their movement is alive and OK in America, but not burgeoning. Under present conditions, I don't expect it to burge on, either. We're far too addicted to all the snazzy benefits we get with a nice church building and a paid, professional pastor.

I just don't foresee believers in North America swarming into house churches. And that's why I don't really promote them. But hey, don't let *me* stop you! I like house churches. If they were good enough for my role model Eutychus, they're good enough for me.

Be Conservative When You're Being Radical

Seriously, if you now find yourself in a church that is already planning to convert to the house church model, congratulations. This book won't affect your church much except perhaps to give it a tiny push over the line. But let me mention a couple of things in closing.

First, unity in the body of Christ is more important than almost anything else. *Never break that unity.* The church is *His* body, and you have no right break it up to further your agenda.

Second, if your leadership is planning on dismissing the pastor, I would urge second thoughts. Instead, consider asking him to focus just on counseling, mentoring, and building up individual believers, especially the men. Shepherding the sheep is a very scriptural task for a pastor. Or you may wish to offer him a sabbatical and keep the door open for future service.

The message of this book is that you don't *have* to sell off the church campus or take every radical step in order to open the church to participation by all. Every church has a different road toward openness. Take a good look around and see how other churches have done it. In Part Four, you'll find a sketch of three churches that are, respectively, top examples in sharing, ministry, and worship.

PART FOUR

How We Did It:
A Tale of Three Churches

13
22 Years of Open Sharing

by Ray C. Stedman

What happens when a church in the twentieth century begins to
operate on these principles? Will they work today as they did in the
early church? The answer is a resounding Yes! When Jesus said,
*Upon this rock I will build my church; and the gates of hell shall not
prevail against it* (Matt 16:18 *KJV*), he had all the centuries in view
until his return. Dr. E.M. Blaiklock, Professor of Classics at Auckland
University in New Zealand, has said, "Of all the centuries, the twentieth is most like the first." Once again, Christians are a small minority in the midst of a despairing and pagan world, and they are
confronted on every side with violence, hostility, ignorance, wide-
spread immorality, and existential despair. They are thus thrust back
into the very climate of the first century where the events and triumphs
of the book of Acts occurred.

As we have seen, the Christianity of the book of Acts is not unusual Christianity—it is normal, usual, typical Christianity as it was
designed to be. The sterile formal, doctrinaire Christianity of our
times is the distortion, with its coldness, its narrow rigidity, its per-
functory ritual, and its bland conformity. Every century has had its
distorted forms of Christianity, but every century has likewise known
something, at least, of the vital transforming power of Jesus Christ
at work through his body. That power has been manifested in the
twentieth century also, strongly at certain times and places, much
more weakly elsewhere, depending on the degree to which individual
churches have either deliberately or unwittingly conformed to the
biblical pattern of operation we have been discovering....

With considerable reluctance I now turn to the experience of a single church in order to demonstrate from real life how well these principles do in fact work in this modern world. The church I have in mind is the one in which I have been privileged to be a pastor-teacher since 1950. It is the Peninsula Bible Church, located on the San Francisco peninsula, at Palo Alto, California. I am fully aware that there are many other churches in the world which could serve as illustrations of the principles we have studied, and doubt-less some of them would be much clearer and better examples than the Peninsula Bible Church. But my limited experience forces me to write only of the church I know best, known familiarly to its members as PBC.

I must also make clear at the outset that by no means is PBC a perfect church. We have made many mistakes through the years and some of them have been grievous indeed. We are still very much learners, being led along by the Holy Spirit into continually unfold-ing vistas and clearer understanding of the principles we seek to fol-low. We have learned much from the experience and teaching of others, and feel most keenly our debt to members of the body else-where for their deeply needed ministry to us. Compared to many other churches around we have found what many regard as an enviable plateau of success; but compared to the New Testament standard, we often fall very far short, and can perhaps be best described by the word of Jesus to the church at Philadelphia in Asia Minor: *Behold, I have set before you an open door, which no one is able to shut; I know that you have but little power, and yet you have kept my word and have not denied my name* (Rev. 3:8).

PBC was begun by five businessmen in 1948, who, with their fami-lies, felt the need for a warmer time of informal fellowship and Bible study than they were obtaining in the churches they were then attend-ing. They did not have any intention whatsoever of beginning a new church, but merely wished to supplement the spiritual diet they were getting. To do this they rented a small room in the Palo Alto Com-munity Center and began holding Sunday evening meetings, while they were still attending their own churches in the mornings. It is now possible to look back and see that what they were hungering for was the *koinonia*, the body life, of the early church. This they achieved to a considerable degree and the meetings were so warm and enjoyable that they attracted many others who dropped in regu-larly for the Bible teaching (often by visiting pastors) and the songfests and informal atmosphere.

So acceptable was this ministry that at the end of one year the people approached the five leaders and asked if they would consider having a Sunday morning Sunday School, as well as the evening meeting, since their children needed the biblical instruction which the parents were receiving in the evenings. This was done, and by the fall of 1950 the number of regular attendants, both adults and children, was running around 100 each week. This was more demanding than the five leaders could handle in the limited time available to them, and thus, in September of 1950, through some rather obvious leading of the Lord, I was privileged to come to the group as their first, full-time pastor.

Of all the principles we have discussed in this book, the only one clear to me at the time of my arrival was deep conviction, derived from Ephesians 4, that the work of the ministry belonged to the people and not to the pastor. I was rather vague as to what that ministry was, but felt from the first that my task as pastor was to unfold the word of God in its fullness, as best I could understand it, and leave to laymen the major responsibility for visitation of the sick, presiding at and leading church services, and evangelizing the world. We determined from the start that we would do no direct evangelizing in the regular services of the church, or within the church building, but all evangelization would be done in homes, backyards, rented halls or other public meeting places....

The third area of unique development is that of the Sunday evening Body Life service. This has attracted so much attention that several Christian magazines have made mention of it and one, *Christianity Today*, ran a special column describing the meeting, in their issue of May 21, 1971. By special permission of the magazine, we will close this chapter with that description.

It happens every Sunday night. Eight hundred or more people pack into a church auditorium designed to seat comfortably only 750. Seventy per cent are under twenty-five, but adults of all ages, even into the eighties, are mingled with the youth, and people of widely varying cultural backgrounds all sit, sing, and pray together.

A leader stands at the center front, a microphone around his neck. "This is the family," he says. "This is the body of Christ. We need each other. You have spiritual gifts which I need, and I have some that you need. Let's share with each other." When a hand goes up toward the back of the center section a red-haired youth runs down the center aisle with a wireless microphone. It is passed down the pew to the young man, who stands waiting to speak. "Man, I don't know how to start," he says, his shoulder-length hair shining as he turns from side to side. "All I know is that I've tried the sex trip and the drug trip and all the rest but it was strictly nowhere. But last week I made the Jesus trip—or I guess I should say that He found me—and man, what love! I can't get over it. I'm just a new Christian, but man, this is where it's at!" A wave of delight sweeps the auditorium, and everyone claps and smiles as the leader says "Welcome to the family. What's your name?"

Other hands are waving for recognition. The leader points to a well-groomed, attractive woman in her mid-thirties. "I just wanted to tell you of the Lord's supply to me this week," she says into the mike. She is a divorcee with small children. Her income had dwindled to the point that she'd had only forty-two cents to eat on that week. But unsolicited food had come. The family had eaten plenty, and she wants to share her thanksgiving. Another enthusiastic round of applause.

Then a sensitive-faced girl with waist-long hair: "I just want the family to pray with me. My brother's blowing his mind with LSD, and it's killing me to watch him coming apart, but we can't get him to stop."

"Phil, go over and stand by her and lead us all in prayer for this real need," the leader requests. "You were in LSD, you know how it feels." A tall, thin youth with a scraggly beard crosses to the girl, takes the mike. "O Father," he prays, "you know how Ann feels and you know how her brother feels. Show him the way out, through Jesus, and show him that you love him just the way he is." He goes on, his prayer eloquent in its simple earnestness, the whole audience listening quietly, with bowed heads.

Then a clean-cut college boy is on his feet, his Bible in his hand. "I just want to share something the Lord showed me this week." For five minutes he expounds a verse from the first letter of John, and the crowd laughs with delight at his practical application.

Other needs are shared. One blond youth asks for prayer that he might be able to buy a car cheaply so he won't have to depend on hitch-hiking to get to his college classes on time. When the prayer is finished, a middle-aged housewife stands at the back and says, "I don't know how this happened, but just this week the Lord gave me a car I don't need. If Ernie wants it, here are the keys."

She holds up a ring of keys, and the crowd applauds joyously as the boy runs to pick up the keys.

Then an offering is announced. The leader explains that all may give as they are able, but if anyone has immediate need he is welcome to take from the plate as much as ten dollars to meet that need. If he needs more than ten, he is warmly invited to come to the church office the next morning and explain the need; more money would be available there. While ushers pass the plate, a young man with a guitar sings a folk song that asks, "Have you seen Jesus my Lord? He's there in plain view. Take a look, open your eyes, we'll show him to you."

After the song someone calls out a hymn number, and everyone stands to sing it together. Then the teacher for the evening takes over. There is a rustle of turning pages as hundreds of Bibles are opened. For perhaps twenty-five minutes the teacher speaks, pacing the platform, Bible in hand. He illustrates with simple human incidents, some humorous, some sobering. The crowd is with him all the way, looking up references, underlining words, writing in the margins. A few hands are raised with questions on the study. The teacher answers briefly or refers the question to an elder or pastor in the congregation. Then the people stand for a closing prayer. They join hands across the aisles and sing softly, "We are one in the Spirit, we are one in the Lord."

When the meeting is dismissed, few leave. They break up into spontaneous groups: some praying, some rapping about a Bible passage, some singing quietly with a guitar, some just visiting and sharing with one another. Gradually the crowd thins down, but it is a good hour or more before everyone is gone and the lights are turned out.

The gathering is called a Body Life Service, a time for members of the body of Christ to fulfill the function of edifying one another in love. It began in January of 1970 when the pastoral staff of Peninsula Bible Church met to discuss the spiritual status of the church. Concern was expressed about the Sunday evening service, which at that time followed a conventional pattern of song service, announcements, Scripture, special music, and preaching. Attendance was rather sparse, running about 150-250 with only a handful of youth present. The major concern was whether we were fulfilling the admonition of Scripture to "bear one another's burden, and so fulfill the law of Christ." Other texts haunted us, such as, "Confess your faults one to another and pray for one another that you may be healed, [admonish] one another in psalms and hymns and spiritual songs." Where was this occurring among our people? Where could it occur?

We determined to make a place for this ministry by wiping out the traditional structure of the evening service and using the time to invite a sharing of needs and gifts by the people. We began with the question, "Where are you hurting? Not where did you hurt ten years ago, but now, where are you right now?"

Predictably, it was slow getting started, but soon a climate of honest realism began to prevail. When that was noised abroad, without any particular invitation youth began to appear—many long-haired, barefoot, and in bizarre dress. Our middle-class saints gulped at first but were determined to be genuinely Christian. They welcomed the young people, listened to them, prayed with them, and opened their hearts. The kids did likewise.

The numbers increased by leaps and bounds. For over a year now it has been going on with no sign of a let-up. Every service is different. Love, joy, and a sense of acceptance prevail so strongly that awed visitors frequently remark about a spiritual atmosphere they can almost scoop up in their hands. *Koinonia* has come![37]

That is part of the impact of one church which has begun to operate on the principles of ministry found in Ephesians 4. Other churches, elsewhere, are experiencing similar blessings, though the emphasis varies from place to place because of regional and cultural differences. Wherever a church is ready to take Ephesians 4,

---

37. Ray C. Stedman, "The Minister's Workshop," *Christianity Today*, Vol. XV, May 21, 1971

I Corinthians 12 and Romans 12 seriously, the Lord of the church
is ready to heal and to bless....

From the Afterword, written in 1976

The Sunday evening Body Life service at PBC was born as the
decade of the violent sixties faded into history and the more hopeful
year of 1970 came into being. At a New Year's Eve service, held till
midnight December 31, 1969, the sharing of the people was so warm
and moving that the pastoral staff, meeting the next week, asked themselves, "Why can't we have meetings like this all the time? How can
we perpetuate this beautiful spirit of love and mutual ministry?" Out
of those questions a determination grew to have a service where the
people could bear one another's burdens and confess their sins and
pray for one another as the Scripture commanded. The latter part of
chapter 12 describes such a service as it was in early 1971.

But what is it like now, six years later in the late fall of 1976 when
this is being written?...

To begin with, the services are still going on. Every Sunday
evening between 6:30 P.M. and the opening time of 7:00, long lines
of cars wait to turn into the parking lots. The proportions of youth to
those over twenty-five have probably risen a bit, to roughly eighty
percent under twenty-five, twenty percent over. The adult portion
still includes men and women of all ages, some well into their sixties
and seventies. A fair number of visitors are always present, on occasion representing as high as ten percent of the total congregation.
Attendance remains almost constant—on rare occasions dropping to
750-800, but usually in the 900-1000 range. The service is still totally unadvertised and the elders have still thought it wise not even
to mention in the church bulletin what the subject for the evening
teaching will be or who will be leading, lest attendance be stimulated
beyond what the facilities can handle.

One noticeable change has been in the music. The guitar still reigns
as king, but the hard-driving rock bands of the early seventies are
seldom ever heard. The folk rock songs of John Fischer, Marge
Snyder and Pam Marks are still popular, but the church hymnbook is
used much more now and some of the great old hymns of the church
are now favorites.

The teaching period is still central to the whole service. A panel
of skilled and capable teachers (many of them in their late twenties
or early thirties) has been developed and the Scriptures are expounded

regularly with great interest and effect. More and more often the sharing period is being spontaneously tied to the passage expounded and a very practical ministry of application and exhortation grows out of the teaching time.

The sharing time itself is still the most distinctive feature of the Body Life service. Almost always it is this which either gives to all who attend a consciousness of love and a deep concern or fails to give it, depending on whether the sharing is deep and genuine, or shallow and artificial. The thirty to forty minutes devoted to this at each service is never adequate for the number of those who want to share. When the leader recognizes an individual out of the number of hands raised, a wireless microphone immediately brought to him makes it possible for everyone to hear all that is said. The leader retains a live mike for himself in order to enter into dialogue, if necessary, with the one sharing. All types of needs, both spiritual and material, are shared and each one is prayed for and often on-the-spot arrangements are made to meet the needs expressed.

Because this sharing time does more than anything else to convey to all present the reality of the church as the body of Christ, it is also (along with the teaching ministry) under sharp and subtle attack from the enemy. Many churches who have attempted Body Life services have found them to take off with a roar, but soon simmer down to a degree of sameness (and dullness) and finally peter out without a whimper. The reason is largely because sharing has been allowed to follow its own course without adequate leadership or guidance and so the enemy has managed to destroy it without a struggle.

It is, of course, the business of leadership to lead. The experience of years has taught us that the key to a successful Body Life service is largely in the hands of the emcee of the meeting. He is to be far more than simply a conductor, keeping everything in order while allowing the meeting to take whatever course it will. He must, in addition, be aware of what will eventually kill the spirit of a service and be very sensitive to recognize those dangerous trends when they begin and to move with graciousness and yet firmness to eliminate them. The delicate balance between sensitive leadership and the autocratic hand of overcontrol, is something only the Spirit of God can produce, but it is an absolute essential to a continuing and fruitful Body Life service.

Within the first year of conducting a Body Life service we came to recognize three factors which are guaranteed to kill the service within a very short time if allowed to go unchallenged. These factors crop up continuously. One or two appearances can be allowed to pass without danger, but they seem to be very infectious and, if not halted by the leadership, will soon take over the sharing and turn the meeting into dull unreality.

The first of these we call "superficial sharing." It refers to sharing trivial matters rather than the real burdens with which people are wrestling. To ask people to pray for nice weather for a fishing trip or that you might find your lost pencil or to get a good grade on a test is to misuse the purpose of Body Life sharing. The same passage which bids us to *bear one another's burdens* (Gal. 6:2) goes on in 6:5 to say, *For every man shall bear his own burden (KJV).* Two different words are used for *burden* in this context. The first one means a burden of great weight, too heavy for anyone to carry alone. The second use refers to a much smaller load which any healthy person should be able to handle without help.

Superficial sharing usually occurs when an individual is afraid to risk anything of real depth. It can arise from pride, which seeks to maintain status and does not wish to appear weak or a failure. It can come from fear that whatever is shared will be met with condemnation or rejection or that it will make him a laughingstock. Or it can come from a lightweight view of life that regards every little problem as the legitimate concern of the whole body. Whatever the cause, it is the business of the leader to discern what lies behind the symptom of superficial sharing and to give instruction that will make possible a true and proper sharing of real burdens. We have found that one of the helpful things a leader can do is to ask the question, "Where do you hurt?" True burdens are those that cause real hurts, and that is what is meant to be covered by the exhortation, *Bear one another's burdens.*

Somewhat similar to superficial sharing and the second factor that is guaranteed to kill a Body Life service, is what can be termed "secondary sharing." Since the sharing of personal hurts is apparently risky to many, they find they can still participate by sharing someone else's burden. "Please pray for my Aunt Mary in Florida. She has just found out that she has cancer and is very frightened of death." This, of course, is a perfectly legitimate source of concern but it is the kind of concern which every person present probably has, and if they all began to share other people's hurts there would be no bearing of their own burdens.

Sometimes, of course, the one voicing such a concern is so intimately involved with the one for whom prayer is requested, or is torn himself by the burden the other bears, that such a request represents a legitimate burden. Often our emcees will ask someone who shares another's burden, "How is this affecting you? Do you feel hurt by this threat to your friend's welfare?" When the individual's personal concern is voiced, the subsequent prayer includes both the need described and the one who voiced it. It is not always easy to distinguish between legitimate burdens for others in desperate need and the use of such to avoid sharing one's own pressing hurt. But Body Life leaders must understand that once secondary sharing starts it is difficult to stop, and yet if allowed to continue it will move the meeting toward dullness and sterility.

The third area of danger is that of "inadequate response." The first, most needed, and yet easiest response to give to a burden shared is to pray for it. This should always be done and preferably by someone who can identify with the problem or need or who has gone through it himself. Prayer must never be permitted to degenerate to shallow and cliché-ridden response. The Apostle James outlines such an instance: *Suppose a brother or sister is without clothes and daily food. If one of you says to him, "Go, I wish you well; keep warm and well fed," but does nothing about his physical needs, what good is it?* (Jas. 2:15,16, *NIV*). In such an instance, even to add "I will pray for you" is hardly a cut better than the answer James records. Such a situation requires action—now!

At PBC we often get requests for help in finding jobs, counsel in overcoming bad habits, need for physical help in moving or meeting some extra demand, requests for financial assistance, etc., etc. To simply pray for these and pass on to some other request is almost insulting. A sincere effort must be made to go further. Here the total resources of the total body must be called into play. Nothing is more exciting than to see how quickly such needs can be met when the whole body is invited to participate. We have seen jobs provided right on the spot; doctor's services donated; financial counselling arranged for; cars given to those without transportation; unmarried mothers-to-be taken into homes till their babies come; alcoholics and drug addicts given help; many food supplies given; baby-sitting services supplied for working mothers, and so on. To actually see these needs being met right before their eyes gives to everyone present a sense of excitement and of the reality of Christian love and concern. Care must always be taken that none of these responses be abused or over-indulged, but it is the duty of elders to exercise just such care, and nothing will deliver an elder more surely from business-as-usual blahs than to experience involvement in the human stream of need and care.

Though the Body Life service itself is still vital, real, and deeply involved with human need, as the preceding paragraphs describe, still by far the greatest effect it has is to stimulate and encourage such living all through the week and throughout the entire body of Christ. Christians are to be loving, caring thoughtful servants of others—not merely at a Body Life service once a week, but at all times, wherever they are. We seek to remind everyone of this at the Body Life service. It has been most encouraging to see how the spirit of Body Life sharing has spread throughout the body and is practiced frequently through the week. No mention of these experiences is likely to be made, but the God who sees in secret takes note of all and is faithful to remember these labors of love with unusual and unexpected blessing.

How long will the Body Life service continue? We have no way of knowing. If it continues to meet genuine human needs in true Christian love and concern, avoiding the shallow, the superficial and the inadequate response, there is no reason why it should not go on till the Lord returns. If it fails to do so, but degenerates into a mere form, kept alive only by artificial programming and great organizational effort, it would be better to let it die and to allow people to feel its lack till their spirit turns to the Lord in bored desperation and cries out for renewal and healing.[38]

Reprinted from *Body Life*, with permission from Regal Books.

---

38. Update: Dr. Stedman retired and recently passed away, but the body life concept rolls on. In fact, it has spread to all the meetings under the auspices of Peninsula Bible Church. It's no longer just a special feature of one meeting on Sunday night, but a lifestyle for the entire church. —J.R.

14
140 Free Ministries in One Congregation

By Tommy Barnett and Leo Godzich

Phoenix First Assembly of God is a big church. That means BIG, as in more than ten thousand every weekend. That's not dollars, that's people!

Pastors Tommy Barnett and Leo Godzich are part of the reason: two men who know how crucial it is to have heavy involvement by everyone.

How do you preserve any semblance of openness and participation when you're that large? Barnett and Godzich do it by massively involving their people in ministry. Right now, they have 140 official church ministries, and most of them were conceived and founded by lay men and women. They also continue to be run by the laity: over 4,600 of them at last count! That means an incredible 46% or so of their congregation is involved in Christian ministry, a figure that would be good even in a small church.

Phoenix First Assembly has been described as the fastest-growing church in America. As the senior pastor, Tommy Barnett has been interviewed many times about the church's massive results in evangelism and ministry. But he and pastor Leo Godzich agreed to give me some answers about a somewhat different area: Phoenix First as an open church. —J.R.

What does it take to get high involvement out of a church's laymen?

Barnett: You have to realize that deep in the innermost being of every man or woman who loves God, there's an innate desire to do something for Him. That desire has to be encouraged and equipped and released if the church is going to do its job. Many of the pastors we work with from other churches find it difficult to look on each and every member of their congregation as someone who wants to do something for God. But that's the attitude the Lord has toward laymen, so that's the attitude we've got to have, too.

Everyone already agrees that we need more lay involvement in ministry, so this isn't anything new to pastors.

Barnett: Church leaders like to bandy about platitudes regarding laypeople without actually releasing them into ministry. This usually leads to a high level of frustration among people who are laymen because they stop viewing themselves as co-laborers in the Lord's harvest field.

The pastor who doesn't release his congregation and encourage it into effective ministry is a long way from the role model of the New Testament church, where they all broke bread, fellowshipped from house to house, proclaimed the gospel, and "the Lord added daily to the church such as should be saved." The Great Commission won't be fulfilled until the church recognizes its role as the body of Christ. And every living cell of that body has to be doing what it's supposed to do. Every member must be a minister.

Okay, so how do you motivate people to minister?

Godzich: For centuries now, churches have felt that they needed to *motivate people* to do something. While that's true to a certain extent, what's really needed is a change of attitude toward the sheep. If you start with the perspective that every member actually wants to do something for God, the question is no longer one of motivation, but of equipping, guiding, and releasing to do that which the Holy Spirit beckons each one to do.

Then how do you release people into service at Phoenix First Assembly?

Godzich: For us, it's not that hard any more. Because of our local reputation as a place to bring people who need to accept the Lord, there's a constant influx of new people. But also we have a reputation as being involved in the needs of hurting people, building up of the saints, and reaching out to the world in a wide number of areas. Even government agencies refer citizens to Phoenix First Assembly when they can't give answers to requests for assistance. And every

February, thousands of pastors and leaders from around the world come to our "Pastor's School," hoping to glean a secret or two about this empowered congregation. Many leave disappointed to find nothing other than the Word of God put into action! The point is our momentum: because of our reputation, everyone just *expects* to be guided into ministry.

Barnett: There's an underlying principle at work here, though. You have to constantly help people develop their own hunger and thirst after God's righteousness. I accomplish this mostly through sharing my vision. Time after time, I share with the people some specific vision—or just a seed of that vision—trusting that God will nurture it in someone's heart and mind toward fruition.

Godzich: That's exactly the way God clarified a vision in my own life. I had prayed that God would show me an area of ministry, several years ago, where He could use me because He needed someone to undertake that cause. One day, as I was sitting in the balcony listening to Tommy preach, he said that someday soon the Lord would lead our church to minister to the people who were hurting most in society today. As I sat there listening intently, the Lord gave me a very real vision of myself hugging a thinned, emaciated AIDS patient with his family on their knees in the background, crying out to the Lord. And to make a long story short, we at Phoenix First pioneered ministry to people with AIDS in our own denomination nationwide, and since then have helped many other churches in this area with their outreach in the AIDS area.

Could you give us any more examples?

Godzich: Yes, we're very long on examples here! In no particular order, I'd mention:

- The Church on the Street, which was started when a man approached us, saying he'd always wanted to be a street preacher. We bought him a bullhorn. And he turned that bullhorn into an inner-city church!
- The Church in the Wind, an ex-Hells Angels group for motorcyclists
- That's somewhat similar to our ministry to ex-prostitutes, in that it was started by an ex-prostitute who approached us, wanting our backing as she established a ministry to young prostitutes on the streets.
- Radical Youth Invasion. A young man named Steve Peebles wanted to reach out to his inner-city roots, so we sent him out to

reach young people, armed with a sound system, blocks to break (to attract crowds), and the gospel! Steve also works in high schools, giving an anti-drug message and then preaching the gospel nearby in the evenings.

- His Sheltering Wing, a complete-care operation for unwed mothers
- Hurting Parents Ministry, led by George and Geri Maynard, helps parents of problem children.
- The Businessmen's Breakfast, led by David Friend, has seen lots of men get saved.
- Adopt a Family Ministries. David and Peggy Quan had taken in foster kids, and they saw a huge need for church families to invite in needy kids, mainly on holidays, and give them presents and a loving home experience.
- The Holy Rollers, who are "wheel-chairished" individuals led by Sharon Henning. For example, the volunteers in Sharon's team are now working with a young fellow named Randy, who had been beaten and left to die on the streets. No one ever found out by whom or why. He wasn't able to talk or walk, and when he came out of a coma at county hospital, the doctors said he would be a vegetable for life. But now Randy's learning to walk, at times without a cane. The team is working with him by using index cards, and he's starting to make sounds and talk. Bus pastors, assistants, and their workers vie with each other for the privilege of taking Randy home with them for special visits. He's a joy! He wears the physical and emotional scars of the past, but is becoming one of God's brilliant stars. In fact, as of today, he's walking and talking pretty well!
- Overcomers From Alcohol, a support group in the church.
- The Saturday Soul-Winning Society, which is just what it sounds like!
- The Early Childhood Ministry. We're the only church of our size that has a free, co-operative nursery. And our nursery kids start memorizing Bible verses at age two!
- The Clothing Ministry
- Hospital Visitation, which is led by Alvin Booher, who's 88 years old. Last year, he prayed with 7,000 patients in hospitals—and more than 1500 received Christ!
- MOMS—Meals Outreach for Mothers, was started by Lynne Frank. When a new mother in the church comes home from the hospital, MOMS sends her a different woman every evening for

seven days. She gets a good meal, household help, and anointing with oil (olive oil, not baby oil!) as they dedicate mother and child to the Lord.

- The 24-Hour Crisis Line
- Our missions group, M.A.P.S.
- Overcomers, which deals with alcohol, drugs, and co-dependence—co-ordinated by Gene and Carolyn Johnston.
- The Mormon Ministry
- Political Action Ministry
- Prison Ministry
- Son-Beams, Judy Summers' ministry to the handicapped

I could go on. There's the men who carry the cross and preach in the streets, the walkie-talkie preachers, coffee house preachers, Sunday School and women's ministries, and the huge bus ministry.

I've got to mention one incredible turn of events recently. A former AIDS patient who is diagnosed as "hopeless" is now recovering. His witness to the church has been tremendous.

And do your laymen handle everything without pastoral oversight?

Godzich: No. I have full confidence that the Lord tends to His work through the people of God. But this doesn't preclude my responsibility for oversight and guidance as a pastor. We've found that too many times, an untrained "lay" person with a new ministry idea is hesitant or has a lot of negative tendencies procedurally, and that tends to lead to either autocratic operation or a committee form of administration that no longer releases the Holy Spirit, but actually fences the laymen into a Pavlovian model of obedience without creativity.

Well, if you have pastoral involvement then you must have a huge staff to keep up with all this lay activity.

Barnett: No, we only have ten official pastors at this point—which isn't much when you're talking about 10,000 people.

For instance, on one Good Friday weekend, kids from the housing projects and other underpriviledged areas in Phoenix flocked to one of our programs, an Easter egg hunt. There were 33,000 youngsters in several football fields across town. The stadiums were flooded with kids and their parents, and literally thousands received Christ and were followed up under the direction of Jeff Allaway. Counting all those people across town, our church "census" for that weekend

was over 50,000! The release of each member as a minister is what
helps our pastoral staff handle that kind of workload.

And just two days ago, our Easter Pageant effort wound up. We
had fourteen performances, 112,000 attendance, and as of this moment, we've received back 4134 response cards from people saying
they want to receive Christ as Savior.

**This is a very impressive operation. You have a lot of activity
going on. But what would you say is the spiritual basis of it all?**

Barnett: A heart of compassion and the desire to see others set
free from various cares and oppressions. But underlying that is our
vision of a holy and righteous God. Throughout history, any noble
compassion that lost its view of God slipped into compromise and
became a powerless work of mercy—which is fine and dandy, but
has little eternal significance and has been emasculated from any
participation in any present spiritual warfare.

The vision of releasing people into ministry is vital, but putting
legs onto that vision requires an element that's increasingly lacking
in modernized society. The element that sets us apart is commitment,
and that commitment is learned here by emulation and example.
People of God are looking for total commitment, and in most churches
they just don't find the examples of it that they should.

Simply put, I'd say that the challenge of the New Testament church
in our day is *not* one of unmotivated people, but one of a wandering
flock looking for a committed leader who will funnel their energy
and desire into effective work. The church today has misunderstood
Hebrews 10:24: "And let us consider one another to provoke unto
love and to good works." To provoke is not to motivate, but to call
forth. The Holy Spirit *will* motivate the people of God if there are a
few pastors and a lot of lay leaders, men and women, willing to take
committed leadership roles, call forth the rest of the people of God,
and keep their eyes upon the Source of our compassion.

15
Pure Worship—
How They Solved the Mystery of the Missing Jewel: *A Sketch of Bread of Life Ministries*

If worship is "the missing jewel of the evangelical church," as Tozer said, then Bread of Life Ministries is a Lost & Found where evangelicals might go to find it. Their meetings are as Spirit-led as you'll find, and the worship flows from their hearts, intermixed with a wide variety of types of sharing.

Bread of Life is a little church of about 125 in Tulsa, Oklahoma. (*Mailing* address: 4035 East 52nd Street. It may not stay little after this goes into print.)

The members learned to meet in an open format in homes, then switched to a gym-like room and started meeting on Sundays in 1990.

They admit that it took them a long time to learn openness. But half of them had no religious background and half had *too much*—of the hopelessly hidebound kind. So they had to start from square one. "Learning openness" wasn't really the problem; "unlearning closedness" would be closer to it. Discipling former pagans turned out to be easier than discipling pew-hardened Christians!

Bread of Life was started by a friendly soul named Tom Mohn, a former Methodist minister, an announcer for Oral Roberts, and a true gentleman. He has held popular church seminars around the country, and you would think he'd have no problems in starting up a fellowship that would pop into high gear after about one week.

Alas, it was not to be. For reasons unknown to you and me, God sometimes teaches His hardest lessons to those who seem to need them least. Bread of Life floundered in its early years, struggling mightily to overcome a variety of problems stemming from members' backgrounds. Tom tells of sitting in some meetings and biting his lip during twenty to thirty minutes of very dead silence, refusing to stand up and preach just to fill up "dead air time." (Now, that's about as bad as it gets!)

He also steadfastly declined to launch centralized ministries. While encouraging everyone to use the Sunday morning assembly to announce their ministry activities and seek volunteers or contributors, he held that the *elders* shouldn't be announcing such things as an institutional, all-church project that *everyone* should feel obligated to support.

Tom's perseverance has paid off. Today, meetings roll on very smoothly for an average of two and a half hours. (Hey, don't stop reading yet!) The time doesn't drag; meetings are packed with drama, the drama of a stage play being directed by an Unseen Prompter who knows the players and understands the parts they can play that day.

A Meeting of Hearts and Minds

Let's take a look at a recent Sunday morning. Feel free just to skim this for its flavor.

A man starts things off by reading from Isaiah 60:

"Arise, shine, for your light has come. And the glory of the Lord has risen upon you. For behold, darkness will cover the earth and deep darkness the peoples. But the Lord will arise upon you and His glory will appear upon you, and nations will come to your light and kings to the brightness of your rising. Lift up your eyes roundabout and see.... I will make you an everlasting pride, a joy from generation to generation."

They then stand and sing Isaiah 60:

Arise, shine, for the light is come.
Arise, shine, for the light is come,
and the glory of the Lord is risen,
the glory of the Lord is risen,
the glory of the Lord has come,
the glory of the Lord is risen upon me.

...and another song:

Lion of Judah on the throne,
I shout your name, let it be known
that you are King of Kings, you are the Prince of Peace.
May your kingdom's reign never cease!

Hail to the King
Hail to the King
Lion of Judah come to earth,
I want to thank you for your birth,
for the living word, for your death on the tree,
for your resurrection victory.
Alleluia
Alleluia
...and another:
Lift high the banners of love, hallelujah,
Sound the trumpet so full!
Christ has gotten us the victory, hallelujah,
Jericho must fall!
...and another:
For the weapons of our warfare are not carnal, but
mighty through God, through the pulling down of strong-
holds, casting down imaginations, and every high thing
that exalts itself against the knowledge of God. And bringing into captivity every thought through the obedience of
Christ.

After four more songs (they like to sing), a man stands and speaks
for about fifteen minutes on light and darkness, closely following a
series of Scripture verses. The message is punctuated once by the
congregation singing a song. At the end, he prays,
O Father, Jeremiah was right, the heart is deceitful and
desperately wicked. Who can understand it? Who can
discern it? You and you alone, Lord Jesus. You and you
alone are faithful to bring the lamp of the light of God into
every portion of our being, and to fill us with light that
we might be vessels of light.

Another song, and a different man speaks for three minutes on light
and conviction, guilt and repentance. But he concludes, curiously,
with a line from a poem: "On the plains of hesitation bleach the bones
of countless thousands who, upon the dawn of victory, sat down to
rest—and resting, died." ("Or turned off the light," he adds.)

There follows a long silence—during which, I presume, everyone
is trying to figure out the meaning of the poem. Open meetings do
produce interesting side trips.

Another man speaks for a couple of minutes on the need to share
the light as we live in fellowship. A woman speaks briefly on asking God what He wants of us. A man gives thanks for several events

in his life and asks for prayers about his career. In response, someone prays what I think is a refreshing and exemplary prayer, turning a *petition* into *worship*:

...you have loved him with an everlasting love ... you have never withdrawn it, you have never ceased to love him. You have been with him from the moment of conception, for you knew him from before he ever was. You knew him before the beginning began. So Father, we're grateful for the path that he now recognizes by the Spirit that has been your mercy and your love.

Lord, we join with him in his testimony to your faithfulness through the hard times, and we realize that both success and failure in the world's eyes are impostors. We desire that which is full of light and life in Jesus. And our brother stands in the light of your love, and he desires to fulfill that to which he has been called. He desires to give himself to you (and has), Father, and we pray that you will grant your peace of your Spirit that will enable him to make the decision that will bring glory to you.

We trust that you, having brought him thus far, are certainly not going to stand over him and threaten him if he makes a wrong decision. You'll just have to make another of your gracious adjustments! And Lord, you are the Champion Adjuster of all time and space, so that our brother can freely choose a direction ... not trusting *that*, but trusting you. And you shall bring him to the fullness of manhood in Jesus Christ. We thank you for this man of God, our brother. Thank you Jesus.

Another song ("O, Lord, you're beautiful..."), a long pause, then a man goes up to one of the two stationary microphones. He is a pretty tough fellow, a Polish former Catholic from the south side of Chicago. But today, he speaks softly and very, very slowly, as the Lord moves in his heart and he talks about repentance for long-term verbal abuse of his twelve-year-old son. The tone is highly emotional...

"I kept telling myself I don't have to do this. (sigh) I woke up this morning with God's glory all around, and He said 'Do you want to do a funeral today?'

"What I want to share is simple. I'm an angry man. You are seeing the end, like a giant slug that's carried itself since the beginning of my life to this point, and it's going to die right now.

"I have ruled my family, my life, everything that I have, through intimidation and anger. I've ruined myself. I don't know what to say except that I know I'm not alone. This has gone on throughout my entire life. I don't know how other people handle life. But in my family, when anything was tense, or anything built up, or anything happened, if I didn't get my way, it didn't make any difference, I got out on the wrong side of the bed. I was an angry person. I solved all my problems with the energy of anger. And, I'm changing today.

"You're seeing a culmination of something that's been happening for over a year, you're seeing something that's happening now. This is [because of the] dedicated prayers of people who care about me, and have cried together with me, I don't know why, but..." At this point, he falls on his knees and asks forgiveness of his son.

Everyone is gripped by this touching and crucial moment, and many prayers are offered. (Who of us hasn't hurt someone in his family?) One person says...

Lord we lift up this part of our old nature that we're not very proud of. And we say Lord, take it to death; in Jesus Christ, take it to death, Lord. Take it from each one of us as we try to manipulate one another. As the fear that is from within us rises up in the form of anger, we call it sin, and we ask, Lord, that you would deliver it from us, that we might walk in faith and not in fear. That we might be delivered from the need to manipulate, Lord, and that we might truly trust you, and therefore, allow this to die. In Jesus Name."

Again the tune spontaneously springs forth: "Arise, shine, for the light is come...." And another prayer:

"O, Savior, you break every fetter. Savior, Jesus, you break every fetter, and you set the captives free. Thank you Jesus Christ. Thank you Holy Spirit. Hallelujah."

A woman shares about how God has brought light into her life through other Christians. Another woman tells a simple, touching story about how God gave her little daughter a new heart as she simply confessed a sin to her mother. Then a third woman stands and sings a song by herself:

"It's been said in a poem, when snow covers the earth, that it hides nature's scars and gives nature new birth.

And they say, when a man turns from sin to the Lord,
that forgiveness like snow, covers him evermore
And somewhere it's snowing, see the soft coming down,
as the snowflakes surrender to the hardening ground,
as the good grace of Jesus that now covers our sin,
in the kingdom of heaven ... its snowing again!
The singer adds, "I just felt like it snowed this morning. I praise the Lord."

A man comes to a microphone. (About seventy per cent of the messages and sharing at Bread of Life come from men.) "You know what a fetter is, don't you? When you fetter a horse so it can't walk, it's hobbled. Well, all of us have got things that have fettered us, that have bound us. And Jesus breaks every fetter. It's an old chorus and it goes like this: "Jesus breaks every fetter..." And he leads the song.

Another man relates a thought from Hawthorne's *The Scarlet Letter*, telling how sin can destroy us unless we bring it into the light.

Perhaps in response, a young woman rises to say, "This is only my third time to come here, but I felt very welcome. I've been trying to find God for the past seven months, and I've been to a certain church that is very organized and you couldn't talk and nobody sang very much. I didn't feel anything at all. Since I was seventeen I've cursed God. I cursed Him because I have a brain tumor. I've cursed Him for it, and now I've found that, maybe if I have Him beside me, I can deal with it a lot better. And, I believe Him, but I don't know if I trust Him very much yet. It's hard to say that, but it's honest. I'm learning to trust Him. But I know that He's there, and that's very important to me. I really appreciate this church."

Another lady immediately moves to pray for her, "Lord Jesus, we just thank you for Lisa, and I ask that you would heal that tumor— dry it up in Jesus name. And Lord, I'm so grateful for her candor, her openness. I'm grateful for her tender heart, and I ask, Lord, that you will fill her with your Spirit right now. Let her know that you're not an angry God that's trying to beat up on her. That you love her. You love her so much that you bled for her and you died with her that she might be risen with you. And I ask you to bless her from the top of her head to the soles of her feet, healing every hurt and wound, Lord, and filling her with your love. 'Jesus loves Lisa.' Let it be carved into her spirit and her soul, by the Spirit of God. 'Jesus loves Lisa.'"

With obvious pain, an older woman responds, "Lisa just gave me courage. She's young and I'm old. She's thin and I'm fat. And she's cursed God, and I've followed God, and I've loved God for a long time. But over Christmas, I've been cursing God. I met with an old friend over Christmas. We've been Christians together for a long time. And she's real. We've had little kids together. We've known each other since our kids were tiny, and now her kids are grown up, and she has a life. She rides her bicycle twenty miles a day and has a boyfriend and is a Bible teacher, and I've just been cursing God because I tried to remain faithful to God, and I don't have that something. I don't have a life (which is a lie, but it seems like the truth). And it's just been ripping me apart ... But I know what it is—it's cursing God, and you put it into words, Lisa. And I thank you, and I just repent of that lie, and I just choose to stand with you Lord, no matter how it feels, or what the lies are. I turn away from that cursing you. Forgive me Lord. Thank you for putting this in words."

A long, holy silence.

A man stands and rambles for a minute about his past and his much improved present, then goes on, "I would really like to praise God today for some other blessings that I have. One blessing that has really been difficult to express—I have been so selfish—my blessing in my wife Joan. What a blessing she has been to me. Just her faithfulness to the Lord through all my crap, and my digging in my heels, my anger. My anger with God, my anger with myself—Joan has just pressed me to the Lord. As a lot of you know, that hasn't been easy. He has given us special grace during the holidays because of the loss of our son. But He has also, once again, given us a blessing! Joan and I will have another member of our family, with God's grace, in July. I wanted to share that all with you, and we ask for your prayers. You know Joan needs special care, and the baby does. We just ask for your prayer. We do thank you so much for your faithfulness." The congregation breaks out in applause.

The Rainbow Tapestry

More messages of five to ten minutes. More songs—antiphonal, solos, even chants. More praise. More worship.

And on it goes, from one unexpected contribution to the next, always taking surprise turns and never adding up to anything "typical." With every turn of events, the Holy Spirit weaves together a rainbow of varied hearts and broken lives into an intricate pattern that only He can see ... until that day when the Lord of Mercy surprises us all with the end result: a dazzling tapestry enfolding his bride, the church, and bringing together a ragged tangle of threads into a design so flawless you'd never know it contained anything that was *ever flawed at all.*

And now, here is the fact you must not miss.

Do you have in your mind a picture of this assembly? ... a photo montage of these hearts and minds, reaching out eagerly toward God and each other?

Then just for this moment, imagine *another* picture: this same group, on the same morning, sitting in rows in a traditional church, with no chance to speak, to share, to worship, to support or feed each other in love. What *would they do* with the fire in their hearts? What would become of them?

PART FIVE

The Open Church Is God's Idea

God writes history. At least the parts that are interesting.

Humans, however, have a dickens of a time making out His handwriting. It's not that He writes too small. It's that He writes too big.

Here is a big mega-lesson from history for those who think I'm making all this up as I go along. (Also, see "Back to the Future Church" in the addenda.) You will find three pages of examples from life and history. At first, you'll wonder why I've slowed the pace of the book by bringing in facts "from left field." But the open church requires *far* more effort than the closed church, and if you read thoughtfully, you'll discover that God has showered the earth with vivid examples of why we absolutely *must* see the church as a focus of great effort and not as a nice place to relax on Sunday.

The three pages of golden examples you'll read here may seem unnecessary to some, but I feel that in the crucible of life, where we all tend to take the easy way out, you'll need every one of them to keep your feet steady as you go.

Besides, they reveal the open church as an integral part of God's world, not just one man's idea. If you really knew me, you would realize that the open church is far too large an idea to have sprung from my petite intellect. The open church coincides 100% perfectly with God's favorite themes in the Book of History that He has been writing for thousands of years.

16
The Secret of True Greatness: Taking the Hard Road

Ad Astra per Aspera
(The motto of Kansas: To the stars through difficulties)

As I pen these thoughts with my left hand, my right hand holds a sandwich, that culinary marriage of convenience invented by the Earl of Sandwich who, it is said, was such an inveterate gambler that he begrudged even a brief lunch break, and thus found a way to eat at the gaming table. The Earl foreshadowed the compulsive writer.

The bread is made from sprouted wheat, a bonus much valued by health food nuts. It seems that a kernel of wheat generates high amounts of certain nutrients during the strenuous process of coming alive and bursting through the dark, hard soil into the light and air.

You will think of many parallels to this process:

- Aspiring Arnold Schwarzeneggers pump iron to sprout bigger and better pectorals.
- Colleges demand their victims spend countless hours reading drivel and writing useless papers, knowing it's the only way to get the little dears' brains to develop.
- Surgeons these days often turn their patients out onto the street the moment the ether wears off, knowing that movement and exertion are part of the healing process.
- Millions of immigrants work like men possessed, some of them amassing large fortunes, "so that my kids can afford the things I never had." Over one-fourth of all U.S. males die within two years after retirement because work is the only thing keeping them alive!

Nations and civilizations, if they are lucky, face the same challenge to exert themselves and thus flourish. In fact, *receiving and responding to a challenge or obstacle is the sine qua non of a successful civilization. Without an adequate challenge and response, it will never achieve greatness.* Thus saith History.

Surprising, isn't it? You'd expect some more obvious factor to be the key to national greatness.

Superior racial stock has often been claimed to guarantee a mighty empire. Conquerors from Sargon to Hitler have buttressed their troops with nonsense about inborn superiority, but the argument has proven convincing only at the point of a gun. When cooler heads have prevailed, they have shown that every race produces a few gifted people. They have shown "that half our civilizations are based on contributions from more than one race."[39]

Favorable geography has also been claimed as the cause of the sprouting of an advanced civilization. This hasn't worked out, either. For example, the fertile lower valley of the Nile helped early Egyptian society, but didn't create it. If it had, then the lower valleys of the Jordan, the Indus, the Colorado, and the Rio Grande would have transformed their denizens into at least a semblance of progressive civilization. But they didn't.

And what about lush countries like Malaysia or Western Samoa, where the living is easy? They simply didn't have environments stimulating enough to goad their natives into doing any heavy thought or construction until Europeans came along and influenced them. When all you have to do is pick breadfruit and mangoes off the trees or throw a net into the teeming waters, why bother to do more?

Let's look at just a few more examples of the Heaven-decreed principle that people and nations must receive an adequate *challenge* and produce a successful *response* in order to achieve greatness:

Before history was recorded, the Sahara Desert was a well-watered grassland. When it gradually began drying up, the inhabitants reacted in three ways:

- some stayed, becoming nomadic.
- some retreated south, following the grassline and retaining their primitive lifestyle, which many of them still have.
- the rest moved to the marshes and jungle of the Nile, facing the challenge of taming it, draining it, and building a growing civilization. The first Egyptians!

---

39. See Arnold Toynbee, *A Study of History*. Many of the examples on these two pages are from him.

All three groups thrived, but the Egyptians became strongest. They grew rapidly until their leaders failed to meet the challenge of making a better life for their subjects and drained away all their energy into the human idolatry of the pyramids.

The sub-Sahara tribes multiplied and developed adequate cultures, but no real civilization. Until Europeans arrived, you would have looked in vain throughout Africa for cities, libraries, highways, or even a wheel. You would have drawn a blank in a search for an alphabet, a math system, or a home made of cut lumber. Motivation was the problem, not intelligence. You now have brilliant black doctors and engineers driving their Mercedes-Benzes around Johannesburg. But the cultural decline of sub-Saharan Africa began with evading a challenge.

Humanity has handled other challenges better:

• The Minoans fled the African coastal drought, mastered ocean travel, and established an elaborate bronze age society in Crete that later gave rise to Greece.

• The Mayans tamed a wild tropical forest.

• The Incas brought life to a bleak plateau.

• The Indic civilization flourished in Ceylon (Sri Lanka), but on the *rainless* half of the island, by building an irrigation system.

• The statues on Easter Island prove it was a great hub of Polynesian civilization even though it's one of the most remote points in the world!

• Lot chose the lush plain of Jordan, and it all went up in smoke. Abraham settled for the tougher land of Canaan, and his descendants multiplied like the stars of heaven.

• The children of Israel got out of the slave business (with a little help from You-Know-Who) and got toughened up further by forty years in the wilderness. They then went into farming and ranching in rocky Palestine, far from the fleshpots of Egypt. Even Philistia had better land than Israel, but the Jews achieved greatness while the Philistines struggled.

• But the most electric example of *Ad Astra per Aspera* is in our own United States as contrasted with Spain. Spain quickly found the treasure in Latin America and raped it. Little challenge there. Life was easy in those warm and fertile lands, with slaves to do much of the work. In high contrast, the Pilgrim Fathers who peered out across Plymouth Rock in December of 1620 saw a bleak scene indeed. Their struggle was for survival, not for gold and silver. No fruits or vegetables or livestock awaited them.

The incredible energy and raw horsepower of the Pilgrims and Puritans laid the basis for the mightiest country the world has ever known. (Later Colonists in Labrador failed badly. A challenge *can* be overwhelming.) Years later, when the pioneers opened up the frontier, their massive effort wrote a chapter of history that is still being celebrated in song and on film around the world. It wasn't all pretty (ask any Indian), but no nation ever had a frontier like ours, and the glory of its challenge will never be duplicated. It made us what we are.

Challenges can also have a military dimension:

- After the Assyrians conquered some of their neighbors, they should have accepted the challenge of developing and governing what they had. Instead, they opted for "more of the same." They were hideously aggressive and sadistic. All the dictators of our century wrapped together would not evoke as much fear and loathing as a King of Assyria. In the end, they exhausted themselves by aggression, and their neighbors rose up and destroyed them in a frenzy of revenge and hatred.

- Athens was occupied, its temples destroyed, and its inland region of Attica devastated. All of Attica had to leave and cross the sea as refugees. But in this desperate state, they took on the full power of the mighty Persian empire under Xerxes and defeated his navy at Salamis in 480 B.C. and crushed his army the next year. The spiritual momentum from this immense effort immediately burst forth in an explosion of Greek commerce, architecture, art, philosophy, and literature unmatched in history.

- In our time we have seen how the defeat and shame of World War I spurred the German people to launch an even wider war only twenty years later.

- Japan emerged from World War II in groveling disarray. But their embarrassment spurred them to adopt an ambitious, tightly-controlled plan for mass production of goods (devised, ironically, by American manufacturing expert W. Edwards Deming).

But historians have known all these things for years. What is less noted is that the same principle of greatness applies to churches— and to you.

So why didn't I devote the above pages to *personal* examples? I was afraid you might shrug them off as randomly selected stories that didn't really prove anything about how God works *normally*. **Facing and accepting a major challenge is the only path to greatness God has ever offered a nation, and if you personally expect more**

favorable treatment than Israel, Japan, Athens, and the United States of America, you're in for a long wait. The truth of this principle becomes even more shocking when you realize that God even allows Himself to be subject to it! Not only has He brought glory to Himself through myriad problems in recorded history, but He is even using Satan's challenge to His ownership of the earth to produce many awesome acts of deliverance and redemption for us, His people. As a Christian involved in His work, you're part of God's counter-challenge to Satan's ambitions. You're part of God's underground counter-rebellion, and if *this* challenge isn't big enough for you, I give up!

Now that you've endured this incredibly windy introduction, you're ready for the main point of the chapter, which is...

Take the Hard Road and Thrive

Here's the part your history teacher never told you, the part about how God sorts out winners and losers.

My friend Moishe Rosen, the executive director of Jews for Jesus in San Francisco, has recently come out with a piece of advice that is truly gutsy. (But then Moishe is a gutsy kind of guy.)

He says the entire Christian church should stop shying away from Jews and gear up to train everyone to do Jewish evangelism. Now, that is possibly the toughest kind of evangelism there is, and in order to share Christ with the Jewish people, we'd have to become well prepared indeed. In the process, I think we'd become so well equipped that *ordinary* evangelism would seem as easy as falling off a church steeple. Which is exactly Moishe's point.

God gives us chances for greatness by sending us challenges, either <u>problems</u> requiring patience-faith or <u>opportunities</u> requiring boldness-faith (and maybe a lot of work). We accept God's offers of greatness by obediently facing, accepting, and acting on His challenges, like the nations you just read about.

Unfortunately, we seldom accept these challenges. Or worse, God knows it would be useless to send us a challenge, so He doesn't even bother. He knows we would flee from it if at all possible. So the type of challenges most of us accept are mainly events like a broken leg. Anything optional, no dice. We move heaven and earth to avoid it.

This shouldn't be terribly surprising to you. In our daily lives, you and I make **massive** efforts to arrange everything to be easy as possible for ourselves. This includes anything from putting off household chores to driving cars with automatic transmissions to buying a TV set with a remote channel selector. Thousands of things. And it definitely includes our attitude toward what we do for the church.

Most of us are spiritually lazy. Very lazy, in fact—even if we are hard-working *physically*. Taking the harder of two alternate roads is foreign to us. Of course, there is a sliver-thin minority of Christians who are self-disciplined to the point of being ascetic, but that's less than one per cent of us. Most of us have an inertia problem, and it holds us back from greatness in God's sight.

Laziness of spirit may also be compounded by fear ... or bitterness and resentment ... or coldness ... or worldly values ... or narcissism ... or pleasure addiction ... or lack of endurance ... or tolerating sin ... or pride ... or a few other common ills. Whatever. The end result is the same: an epidemic of mediocrity. Look around you. How many of your friends would you point to as an example of true greatness? How many have taken on the sort of life-transforming challenges that turned the early Nile settlers into Egyptians? or changed African drought victims into the founders of a whole new civilization in Crete? or transformed a sickly band of English refugees into the steel and muscle of the most powerful nation ever seen?

But take heart. The lethargy that holds us back can be mostly erased in a rather short span of time. The open church offers an unending series of challenges to grow into greatness and gain...

A Whole New Quality of Spiritual Life

Want to be a different person? Want to leapfrog over the personal limitations that have held you back all your life?

In an open church, you will have opportunities to grow by the truckload. In the Sunday morning gathering of the saints, you'll have a chance a minute to do things you've never done before. And during the week, you'll be free to minister to others *with the prayers and backing of your entire church* in ways you've not been able to do before. Tasks and challenges that once were beyond you will now be within your reach. It's like being a quarterback on a football team with 300-pound linemen; in play after play, they'll create a hole in the opposing line, a patch of daylight for you to run through. And when you have that daylight, the future is as bright as the promises of God.

You Can't Have Your Cake and Greatness Too

The reason I had to write this chapter is that the closed church service is such a seductive affair.

For the layman-listener, it's a piece of cake. If you can hold down a pew cushion for 60 minutes and move your lips a little during the singing, you've parred the course.

In high contrast, the trouble with the open church is that *it takes more effort by a long shot.* True, it will give you far more spiritual strength and encouragement. True, it will give you numberless patches of daylight to run toward the glory of God. But when you get down to where the Reebok meets the sidewalk, it costs you time and effort—which puts it at a disadvantage to the closed church with its fail-safe services, sure-fire sermons, set-in-concrete policies, automatic-pilot staff work, and professionally-run smorgasbord of programs.

A thoroughly open church may eventually go smoothly, but *never* automatically. There are always surprises, just like any growing family. When anything happens, it's because *you* did something! The worship is in *your* hands. The sharing and caring and training are in *your* hands. The work of evangelism, pastoring, and charity is in *your* hands.

If this sounds a little scary, well, it is. We're talking about your one and only lifetime here on earth, and we're talking about you shouldering the work of Almighty God. This is not a rehearsal, not a game, not a training session for the real thing. This is **it**, camper.

The closed church involves a fair amount of game-playing in the sociological sense, but in the open church, you'll seldom play games; you'll be in action, taking your place in history. And in real history, people and nations have to seize opportunities as they flit by. When you hitch your wagon to the stars of heaven, you may find more than stardust in your path. With every strand of love, you may find a stream of suffering. With every touch of joy, you may find a ton of work—not wearisome toil, but the creative work of building living monuments to the grace of God.

Finally, the Payoff

On page one, I implied that you probably feel lonely and unimportant in church now and then. Was I right?

No matter, I suppose. That's history. You've read this to the end, and that likely means you're serious. You're now planning in your heart to become part of a team of players under God in an open church, am I correct?

Although I don't know you, I'd almost bet you've already made that decision. You're already daydreaming about how exciting your life is going to be. If I'm right in this, then you've just inherited a treasure beyond measure. You'll soon have:

1. *Friends who are close in a way no one else can match,* people who have come to understand you by spending hours listening to you and sharing in depth. They truly appreciate your strengths and are sympathetic with your weaknesses. They give you help when you need it. They laugh with you, cry with you, and never ever turn their backs on you.

2. *Growth in power and maturity.* As part of an open church, you are no longer living on your own power base. You're plugged into a high-voltage circuit of friends who can multiply your strength by a factor of ten, twenty, thirty—even a hundredfold.

3. *Continual challenges.* They don't let you quietly slide downhill. If you start to get flaky, act mean, put things off, or otherwise waste your life, they know you well enough and love you enough to bring you back on track. They give you the kind of help you couldn't hire with ten million dollars.

Soon you will be called upon to do things even your mother never dreamed you could do—and you will do them! ...not because you were born talented, but because The Counselor will be with you in ways you never imagined possible.

I promise you all this and more:

The Spirit of the Lord is the Spirit of Adventure, and the drama of following Him into the unknown will lead you up unexplored footpaths gleaming with golden question marks and sparkling with diamond mirrors in which you can catch occasional glimpses of His face. But still it's a rocky path, and in time it will bend sharply upward into the rugged mountain terrain where you'll have to scramble on your hands and knees, perspiring every inch of the way and trembling in the rare atmosphere. Now and then, you'll even have to take an occasional risky jump across a dark chasm, and you may wish for the safe old days in the flat plains far below you.

But keep responding in faith to every challenge, and at the end of the climb you will find the Lord Jesus Christ himself, the Prince of Glory, walking toward you with arms outstretched and calling out a special greeting for travel-scarred adventurers, *"So you had the courage to take the same unmarked trail I took! Well done, faithful heart, well done indeed!!"*

And perhaps then, in a moment, as you finally stop to rest, you may turn and look behind you, and discover—to your wonder—a thousand others climbing in your steps.

✝ END ✝

AFTERWORD

Let's Stop Playing Church

The time has come to end our 1700-year experiment in spectator Christianity.

Like a doting parent, God the Father is glad to take whatever He can get in the way of worship, but I'm here to tell you He'd be a whole lot happier if for once, just once in his life, Sam Christian were allowed to stand to his feet on a Sunday morning and say, "I love you, Lord. You mean everything to me."

What harm could come from that? Would the walls buckle or the organ explode or what?

I live for the day when Sue Christian can stand up and tell how the Lord changed her life this week. Are only men allowed to testify to God's grace? Would the steeple be struck by fire from Heaven if a woman (say, your mother) were to put in a good word for the Lord without first stepping outside the sanctuary door?

Why can't we, just for a few minutes a week, simply be a family together—God and His kids—doing what good families do: sharing their hearts and lives?

We don't need to turn the church upside down or torch the Sunday school rooms.

But on the other hand, we don't simply need to get better at what we do on Sunday. We're already past masters at listening to sermons and announcements and singing.

What we desperately need is to do something different: to learn to interact in depth with God and each other. And in that, we're still in kindergarten.

No More Business As Usual

We can no longer afford church customs and patterns that turn dreams into hamburger, Sunday mornings into a school-like game, and Christians into ineffectual wimps. Laymen have to start behaving like men again, not standing around and waiting till they're asked to do something.

Why change now? Because the King of Heaven sets the pace, and His pace is jumping toward the moon. For instance, between 1980 and 1990, the percentage of the world's people who are unevangelized plummeted by 8.0%.[40] Amazing!

And yet 65 countries are now "officially closed" to all foreign missionaries (up from zero in 1900) and about four more close each year, forcing us now to launch a massive tentmaker strategy. *If your church is statistically average, the Holy Spirit would like you to send several of your families abroad as tentmakers within the next twelve months.*[41] Believe it!

Because of the power that God is unleashing worldwide, business as usual won't do anymore. And because you now know what an open church can accomplish, business as usual won't do in your life and your church anymore, either. It's too late for you to turn back and forget you ever read all this, even if you wanted to. You must go forward.

Pollster George Gallup recently pointed out another reason you can't go back:

> ...unlike any decade in history that preceded it, the decade of the 1990s will be shaped by the people themselves ... from the bottom up.... We will hear a more persistent voice from the laity, who want a greater role in shaping the church.

Pray

If you're the one who's spearheading the effort to open your church, you need to pray for awhile. An hour or two wouldn't hurt.

Don't bother to ask God to clear the problems out of your path. That's *your* job, pilgrim! But do ask Him for three things: wisdom, power, and love.

Also, it would be very smart to ask for at least one kindred spirit among the church leadership you can pray with and dream with. Lone Rangers don't get very far in the church restoration business.

Whatever you do, don't let your efforts create friction or dissolve into a factional issue. Keep it friendly! Keep it brotherly! Concentrate on telling people about the benefits of an open church and how they'll enjoy the closer fellowship, growing, and learning. I guarantee you that a you-versus-them scenario is the *last* thing you'll want.

The Impossible Is Now Possible

Do all the high goals in this book sound unrealistic to you?

---

40. *Pulse*, March 23, 1990, p.1

41. Global Opportunities (1600 Elizabeth, Pasadena, CA 91104, phone [818] 398-2393) has 105,000 overseas, secular job openings on computer. For a very modest fee, they will match up a mission-minded Christian with exactly the kind of job he desires.

Under the status quo, they would be. But remember, we're talking about a revamped worship service that could transform your people like a cold shower. You won't have many spiritual blobs who show up once a week and then vanish. You'll have people of *action*. Concerned *participants*! Powerful, loving disciples who are taking their places as leaders in the battle force under the Commander of the Armies of Heaven.

So free yourself from deadening, unscriptural church customs and make the Lord Jesus Christ the heart of your church—not just its titular head!

Start Today

Surely at some point in your life you've been in on at least one cottage prayer meeting or other gathering where the atmosphere was hushed and electric with the presence of God, where time stood still and people's whole lives were changed just by being in that presence.

That's the sort of experience within your reach *every Sunday* when you begin to involve your people in a time of open interaction and true worship. It happened in the primitive church, it has happened to me, and it can happen to you.

An open church will revive and transform your laymen like nothing else you can name. And your pastor's life will change gears, too. (I can't absolutely guarantee to get him out on the first tee by one o'clock every day, but I do have his best interests at heart. Trust me.)

Any change in your church must start with *you*. That means you need to start the wheels rolling as soon as possible. Order some more printed material or start talking to people—and by all means, *pray*. If you delay your first step beyond today—well, you're old enough to know what happens to projects you dawdle with! Start talking to people right away: spouse, friends, church leaders, whomever. If you're not up to that yet, practice on the dog.

Using this book—and perhaps a few others—you can probably handle any challenges that come your way, by God's good grace. But if you'd like to explore getting further help from Open Church Ministries, feel free to write for information about seminars, conferences, speaking engagements, or consulting with your church leadership. The address is at the end of the bibliography.

You're off and running! Don't let anything slow you down. Remember, you're on a mission from God.

The Favorite Questions

Q: Ah, but in our church, we have home Bible studies, an answer-back time after the sermon, and a big visitation program for those who want to minister, so we don't really need all these changes you're recommending.
A: You have Band-Aids. You have some excellent programs designed to fill the void that should be mostly filled at 11 a.m. Sunday. *Nothing*, however, takes the place of pure worship. *Nothing* takes the place of true sharing and free ministry among the whole church, where the numbers are large enough to assure the presence of the entire range of gifts. Don't kid yourself; you're missing out on some of the greatest blessings on earth.
Q: Forget it. Our people would be scared to death to try anything like an open church format. Nobody would say anything!
A: If the leadership of the church is truly committed to a Biblical format, it's going to work, somehow. I promise. It's *God's* format, an original New Testament pattern, not just somebody's latter-day brainstorm.

All churches require a period of warm-up, preparation, education, coaching, or whatever. Some more, some less. It's not always easy. There's always a certain amount of resistance to new things. But that's life. Don't run from life. Embrace it. If you spend too much of your time on earth avoiding the difficult options, life turns pale and slides through your hands like water.
Q: Well, you sure haven't met *my* pastor. He squelches anything that looks risky to him, and boy, would this look risky!
A: Before you do anything else, stop and think for a minute about how good-hearted your pastor is and recall the many fine qualities that prompted your church to hire him. Then think about how he might have come to be such a "squelcher":

1. Suppose, for example, you're in a church that's so fundamentalist you don't allow your young people within 200 miles of Bob Jones University. And then suppose one of your church's far-flung programs goes off on a toot where people are (*gasp*) *speaking in tongues*. Just

who do you suppose is going to wind up taking the heat for that? After all, nobody but the pastor would recognize antinomianism or semi-Pelagianism if they tripped over it in broad daylight. Face it, your minister is the designated umpire, censor, and chaperone for everything that takes place in the church, whether he's there or not. This "resident cop" responsibility is supposed to be distributed among your elders, but it just isn't.

2. Suppose he does bring in some open church changes, but with poor preparation—or too little of it. And suppose three or four of the pillar$ of your church react badly and decide to move on down the road. You could be in major financial difficulty. Every pastor's nightmare.

3. I'm afraid your church rather *likes* squelchers. If your pulpit selection committee had wanted a wild-eyed radical, they would have found one in the first place.

4. He already bears ultimate responsibility for your church's 3,726 programs.

I hope all that helps explain why he "squelches everything."

Look, let's state the obvious: Unless your pastor (and elders) eventually come to favor the idea of an open church, it's not going to happen.

But 99% of all the pastors I've ever met were reasonable people, and there are ways to gently bring them around to reality when they're being unduly negative on something. See chapter 9-11.

Q: This is just too much for me. And I think it would be too much for my church to handle at this point in time also.

A: All is not lost. You can implement at least some of these changes. Anything is better than nothing. Anything will get you started in the right direction.

Q: Isn't an open sharing period apt to be taken over by loudmouths and showoffs?

A: No, it's not. In the instances where someone overspeaks, a designated timer (probably female) can restrain him—or buttonhole him afterward. The far bigger problems are:

1. A willingness to share, but only trivial concerns, not the major ones you're struggling with. Like when your kid's smoking crack in the church basement, and you're upstairs whining about your bursitis.

2. Sharing *others'* concerns. "My uncle's neighbor's mother's best friend is in the hospital. Would y'all pray about it right now?" Guaranteed to trash the whole meeting if it catches on.

3. A weak response to the burdens shared by the others in the meeting. When somebody's lost his job, you *don't* just pray, "Lord, bless George." You try to help George—or lay the groundwork for later help—right then and there.

4. Runaway chains of copycat contributions. One person suggests a hymn, and fifty-three others do the same. Or whatever. Even confession of sins can turn into a destructive bandwagon ride if your people

start copycatting instead of being open to the Holy Spirit's leading. They'll start confessing the silliest things you could imagine, just to be along for the ride. Themes in subject matter are wonderful. Mindless tailgating is deadly boring.

There's no way to avoid these four problems. They recur like leaks in a tweed submarine. You can, however, minimize them by printed and oral reminders as often as needed. In your reminders, aim to be clear without discouraging anyone's contributions. A few "problem people" will not get the picture, even after several reminders to the church as a whole; you have to speak to them privately and gently. Perhaps some kind and gentle soul in your church should be asked to exercise that function.

Q: You're being awfully negative about my pastor. We all love him. He's the main sparkplug of my church.

A: Sure he is. But the Lord intends your church to have *dozens* of sparkplugs! The real question is His intention. Along that line, let me give you some quotes from Johnny and Juanita Berguson's booklet, *What Ever Happened to Christianity?*:

"In the Scripture, we see a gift of pastor, but gifts and positions are not the same thing.... In the New Testament, the leadership was raised up from the local church for the local church.... Our current system is based on importing a professional to be the head of the church. If care is not taken, this can discourage the average member from ministry—especially leadership.... If a person really wants to serve God, he/she is encouraged to go to Bible school. Why? Because the church is not prepared or equipped to raise the believer to maturity so that they, in turn, can raise other believers to maturity.... Rather than the church being like a business, it is to be a family. The two, business and family, have different foundations. Becoming part of a family usually happens by birth or through a commitment that springs forth from love. Family commitment is for life and cannot be simply put aside. On the other hand, a business relationship is based upon accepting a job."

On the same subject, Overseas Council President Charles W. Spicer, Jr., writes me that, "North Africa was the strongest region of Christendom until the third century. Today it is nearly totally Muslim and extremely resistant to the Gospel. Why? Because the early church in North Africa failed to train national leaders. They relied on bishops and teachers from Europe. The church failed to survive in North Africa culture because the leadership was foreign." Imagine! If our Third-Century brothers had learned to use local leaders, we wouldn't have Moammar Quaddafi today.

Q: At the start of this book, I thought it was going to be clear and simple. But you've made it awfully complex. Could you just give me a nice précis of what you're saying?

A: Yes, well, life is complex and my florid prose aggravates the murkiness. But I'll try:

When Christianity became accepted and popular, local churches began to erect buildings and hire pastors. This set off a chain reaction of tragedies:

1. Open worship and sharing ceased.
2. Congregations turned into audiences. Participants became spectators.
3. The true "priesthood of the believer" was discarded. Ordinary believers became mere laymen, with no ministry functions allowed in church.
4. Leadership and authority became centered in the priesthood.
5. Overall, the church became a shell of what it was.

Now, 1700 years later:

1. Open worship and sharing sound, to most believers' ears, like a radical experiment best left to some congregation of ex-drug addicts in California.
2. The church is still an audience with many lonely spectators.
3. Ask a typical evangelical Christian to stand up in the Sunday service to exercise some ministry function, and he will hyperventilate until he faints.
4. Modern pastors are overworked and imprisoned in a highly demanding system.
5. Too many laymen live truncated lives: stunted, hurt, sterile, wimpy.

Myriad problems have flowed from the closure of body life to laymen. But because the source of the problems is unitary, so is the solution: opening the church again. Over time, an open church will:

1. Reduce apathy, weakness, fear of witnessing, worldliness, and overactivity to the minimum.
2. Transform laymen from spectators into strong, healthy participants.
3. Restore each person's individual ministry and make him or her unique in the household of God.
4. Free pastors from overwork and enable them to concentrate on making their parishioners grow spiritually.
5. Turn laymen into joyous, loving, holy, wise, and powerful servant-priests who are capable of fulfilling the Great Commission in our time.

So in a nutshell the message is, **Let's open the church to full participation by everyone!**

For Pastors Only:
Suddenly, the Battlefield Has
Changed—and We're Not Prepared

Ever since Babel, the world has been splintered.

But since November 9, 1989, when the Berlin Wall opened, the pieces are being drawn together again by an Unseen Hand—with hair-raising speed and force.

We are living in the **first-ever** worldwide καιρός, a God-driven time of crisis when the ground of society is shifting beneath our feet.

The three bases of society are government, economics, and culture (which hinges on religion).

For the first time ever, mankind is reaching a consensus on the best form of government: representative, multi-party democracies. Reports of reform and revolution are pouring in from the Soviet Disunion to Timbuktu. In the past two years, I've heard of twenty-one from Africa alone!

For the first time ever, mankind is reaching a consensus on the best form of economy: free markets. At the rate we're going, the wave of reform will soon engulf the planet and leave any non-free-market countries trapped in a backwater of poverty.

And for the first time I can think of, almost all the nations of the world have united on a major course of action: combating Iraq.

Even the war of tongues is fading. Although the chaos of Babel is still with us, the English language is rapidly sweeping the world as a second language. If you're a serious student, you *must* know English.

Soon the consensus will be in on the world's culture. Right now, though, it's still up for grabs, and the only four worldwide religious forces capable of leading it are Christianity, Islam, the New Age, and humanism. Here are the main factors working against each of them:

1. **Islam**

Although it has a strong hold on its people, It's dictatorial, which puts it on a collision course with free markets, free voting, and a high-tech communications web that transmits doubt, decadence, and pluralism directly from satellites to Muslim TV sets.

2. New Age

Although the New Age is aided by TV, Hollywood, and the environmentalists, you can discount it because it's anarchic and lacks a driving organizational force. Besides, it's based on Hinduism, which has never accomplished anything.

3. Humanism

This is the incumbent culture of the West. But secular humanism is doomed because, as Gary North recently noted in *Christian Reconstruction* (Vol. XIV, No. 3):

> The collapse of Marxism is symptomatic of a far more crucial collapse. Marxism's demise is the first stage of a much more significant transformation: the collapse of Western humanist culture.

4. Christianity

That leaves us chickens. You and me. Plus half a billion other Great Commission Christians.[42] Unfortunately, any study of church history strongly reminds us of Pogo's famous conclusion, "We have met the enemy, and he is us."

The war has shifted gears. It's now a battle for the entire planet's faith, and it's coming our way. There will be heavy casualties. (Barrett projects 500,000 Christian martyrs a year by 2000.)[43] We must get our act together and prepare the church for action or suffer badly for our unwillingness to discern God's hand in this kairos.

Why might we suffer? Partly because the blood of many martyrs may be required to crack the Muslim curtain. But mostly because we're not ready to handle the challenges of rapid growth. The closed church system is so slow-moving that it takes years to prepare one new convert for a major work of ministry. Compare that to St. Paul's record of creating viable churches from scratch throughout Galatia, Asia, Achaia, and Macedonia *between A.D. 47 and 57,* about ten years! With no New Testament (which he was busy writing).[44]

When God Strikes, Get Ready for Action

When the Lord of History strikes down a great nation, brace yourself for action. Prepare for massive changes.

Let me mention a few instances from the past.

---

42. "Great Commission Christians" is a handy new phrase from the Statistics Task Force of the Lausanne Committee for World Evangelization. The estimate of 500 million is by Barrett, and Ralph Winter of the Center for World Mission.

43. David Barrett, *Cosmos, Chaos, and Gospel: A Chronology of World Evangelization from Creation to New Creation* (1987).

44. If you think the comparison unfair, see Roland Allen's *Missionary Methods: St. Paul's or Ours?* (Eerdmans, $5.95)

Why did **Classical Greece** collapse so quickly? It was an ungodly but pretty wildflower that bloomed gloriously from about 500 to 323 B.C. and then died.

The root answer is that God was through with it. He let its culture and language develop into the most advanced in the world, but He was mostly interested in using its rich language to carry the complex, subtle message of the New Testament. The rugged and sparse Hebrew language would have been an Excedrin headache to translate into Earth's thousands of tongues.

So in 146 B.C., He let it crumble—and fed its remains to Rome for lunch. Today, "the glory that was Greece" is a distant memory sighed for by anti-God intellectuals who have no other conceptual foundation to build upon. Today, "the reality that is Greece" is a permanent basket case where no responsible mother would dream of sending her youngster to school without a charm pinned to an undergarment to ward off the "evil eye."

Why 4 B.C.?

Why wasn't Jesus born a century sooner or later? Did God like the weather in 4 B.C., or what?

The answer is God's kairos for **Rome.** In 4 B.C., Caesar Augustus (a proxy for Satan) plunged the civilized world into a depth of subjugation and despair it had *never known before*. **For the first time ever**, the entire Western World was administratively controlled by one power—under the aegis of Satan.

Caesar's decree that everyone should be registered—for purposes of dominance and universal taxation—sank humanity's hopes to a new all-time low.

At that point, God struck back *immediately*. One of Rome's victims was a very pregnant Mary, who ironically was forced to Bethlehem, the long-prophesied birthplace of the Messiah (Mic. 5:2). Four B.C. was "the fullness of time."

Rome built a colossal system of roads and bridges, then set up no-passport-required sea lanes spanning the empire, the idea being to enrich the empire and move troops fast to squash resistance. But when Satan freaked out in A.D. 70 and had Titus destroy Jerusalem, scattering the church six ways from Sunday, God used all that nice Roman infrastructure to establish His church all over the map.

Satan's few days of amusement at Jerusalem turned out to be his worst strategic disaster in the New Testament. It seems the Devil is badly overrated as a planner.

Let's Hear It for Marx and Mao

Today, God is overturning nations again, but this time it includes the West *and* the East. It's time to prepare ourselves for changes on a massive scale we've never considered before.

Russia was never exactly famous as an evangelical hot spot. But thanks to Mr. Marx, it is now!

The former evil empire has quickly turned into an overwhelmingly huge, red-hot mission field which is so vast that the Western church hardly knows where to start. The Macedonian calls are reverberating like a 100,000-voice choir.

And let's hear it for Chairman Mao, without whom China would have remained the impenetrable morass that buffaloed missionaries for 85 years. Although Satan moved Mao to slaughter tens of millions of Chinese, Mao did construct roads, radio stations, etc., and simplified the alphabet for type-setting purposes.

So guess who's going to be using all that in a few years. Us, that's who.

Very roughly, there are now 50 million believers in China, counting children. In other words, for every Chinese slain by Mao, there is now at least one Christian. And you ain't seen nothin' yet.

Did God lose control at Tien An Men Square? No way. According to a report in the February 3, 1990, *World*, "In at least seven cities... students have indicated... that as many as 10% of entire student bodies have converted [since the June 4 massacre]. In some cases entire dorms or even faculties have all become Christians."

One lecturer at Xiamen University said, "I would defy anyone to walk from one building to another on this campus and not bump into a group of students having a Bible study in the open air." If that doesn't excite you, check your pulse!

Stop the Kairos, I Want to Get Off

We're nowhere near prepared to handle the Soviet breakup opportunity. And when Red China turns green, we'll be even less prepared to handle that one.

No surprise here, though. When MacArthur appealed to the church to send a host of missionaries to the broken and receptive people of Japan, the church yawned. And today Japan is an economic giant with a spiritual vacuum for a heart.

Maybe I'm unduly pessimistic, but it looks from here like we're preparing to foul up again.

The problem is not a shortage of planning. *Glory!* Have we ever got plans! Out of the 78 plans to evangelize the world that I mentioned before, 33 of them are backed by organizations spending over a *billion* dollars per decade. Each.[45] (It will not surprise you that many of them are sponsored by parachurch organizations, which are not weighed down by the same set of limitations that your church is.)

Just one gargantuan flaw in all this. Whether a plan is sponsored by a church or a para, it's all the same. For both the outreachers and the new

---

45. Barrett and Reapsome, *op. cit.*, p.42.

converts, the moment of truth inevitably arrives: The hour comes when the believer marches in and plops himself in a pew.

Sooner or later, every participant in every brilliant plan wends his way to church. That's where the road slopes softly downward, winds through a maze of liturgical loop-de-loops, threads through a thicket of theological lint, and peters out in a pool of ecclesiastical inertia.

They walk in as plain folks, we turn 'em into an audience.

To compensate, we have a zillion programs, from Bible studies to junior high scavenger hunts, and many of them are helpful. But as a whole, they don't keep people growing long term. People plateau. For 95% of them, spiritual growth slows to a snail shuffle within two years. (You can quibble with these numbers, but in your heart you know I'm approximately right. The slowest-growing thing on earth is a deep sea clam, which takes about 100 years to grow one-third of an inch, but you and I have met some pew-sitters that aren't growing much faster!)

The Main Point

Seems like everybody is praying for a big revival in the '90s.

I'll overlook the annoying fact that many revivals of the past started with a confession of sin in church, and today we don't even have a slot in the service where people could confess to overtime parking.

My point is simple: **If we _do_ get that rapid 1990s growth we've all been praying for, there's no way in the world we'll be able to handle it with a closed-church system where things tend to revolve around the pastoral staff.**

There's no way we'd be able to grind out seminary grads fast enough to fill the pulpits and feed the converts. We've simply got to find more feasible, Biblical, timely ways to create those who can minister.

There's no way we'd be able to build church plants fast enough. We've _already_ got scads of young urban churches meeting in warehouses because they can't get a permit or pay for a traditional church plant.

There's no way we'd be able to give millions of converts a chance to lead in worship and ministry on a regular basis and find their niche in the assembly of faith without the traditional long, slow period of "foundation-laying" that would kill their momentum. Except for celebrities, we dump all new converts into the "not ready for prime time" category for quite a while, sometimes five to ten years.

That's not a speed bump, it's a penalty box.

The same roadblock has shown up overseas. Dave Walz of New Tribes Mission says they have discovered that when using traditional structures (externally-trained executive pastors, buildings, no plurality of leadership), it takes ten or more years to establish a church. With new, open structures, it usually takes two years—during which time they often send out their own missionaries!

It's Time to Update the Church

One of the most advanced Christian strategists of today is Jim Moats, president of Issachar Frontier Missions Strategies in Seattle. I'd like to give you some quotes from one of his recent newsletters (*Strategic Times Journal*, Vol.4, No.3) to point up how out-of-date some of our American church trends are:

"The American village-church of the late eighteenth century was designed with the following in mind:

- 3,200 hours of labor annually were required to feed and clothe the family.
- The geographical sphere of influence was limited to the village or county.
- The typical church member was educated through the eighth grade and lived on a farm.
- The church was clergy-centered and usually located in a rural setting.
- Communications about the fall of the Soviet Union government would have taken months to filter down to the rural church....

"Our church missions committees are managed by a group of dedicated lay people.... The primary purpose of this committee is to manage mission policy, raise money, and fund mission agency operations. This model for missions began in the late eighteenth century when most churches were village-based churches. Several churches pooled their very scarce resources and formed the first mission society, known as the Baptist Mission Society.

"During this period, Christianity was limited primarily to Europe and America. Nearly all mission fields were pioneer in nature and required many years of sowing prior to harvest. Contrast this with the fact that today, only a handful of nations are without an organized Christian presence....

"...while restricted access nations (RANS) of the world are becoming creative access nations (CANS), and open to unique mission endeavors ... the American church is pouring itself into church growth seminars and pastors' conferences. The American church remains frozen in its steps and unable to break out of its past. With each new program comes short-term hope followed by the dismal recognition that nothing under the sun seems to work. When one church experiences significant growth, it immediately attracts the attention of dozens of pastors asking for the golden keys to church growth....

"According to Carl George, Executive Director of the Charles E. Fuller Institute of Evangelism and Church Growth, American churches initiate several strategies to build attendence. The following are some examples: miracle ministry, high visibility events, direct mail, guest speakers, performances, TV and radio ministry, and preaching and revival events....

"At a recent seminar on baby boomers in the church, Dr. Elmer Towns stated that Americans born after WWII are experience-based in their search for fulfillment. He further stated that they have these characteristics:

- They want Christianity to be functional
- They have very high expectations
- They are a generation of competitors
- They only want to play on winning teams and expect to win
- If their church experience feels good, they will stay
- If their church experience is pragmatic and functional they will become involved
- They judge morality by how the church is run more than just the doctrine of the church
- If the church will not help them function, they will not attend and will not serve....

"It is clear that the American church is no longer growing. Certainly there are individual churches that have high levels of growth, but most of these are resulting from transfer growth or reactivating people who attended church in the past. The rate of growth in our missions giving is dropping off dramatically, and is projected to begin losing ground in the coming years. If scores were kept, we would most likely find that the American church is no longer an attractive option in our society. Why is this?

To understand the answer, we need only evaluate ourselves against our earlier comments regarding the characteristics of the Baby Boomer generation.

- Is Christianity, as demonstrated by the lives of churched Americans, functional?
- Are the high expectations of these people being met?
- Are they challenged in practical ways that can draw them into an active, world-changing Christianity?
- Are they being invited to play on winning teams, or are they being asked to sit on the sidelines while other professional Christians play the really important roles?
- Is the church operated on biblical principles or is it a franchise operation from the blueprints of the village-based church?
- Is the church helping them function offensively in a world that is asking them to run in the rat race at a faster and faster pace, or is the church simply trying to steal some of their time from the world for church duty?

Any church that can answer all of these questions positively will be teeming with life and new growth."

The Big Plans for the 1990s

As soon as participation becomes a trend and the church turns its listening laity into participants with clear spheres of ministry, we'll be playing a different ball game.

Today there are 500 million Great Commission Christians worldwide and 3.4 billion people who don't claim to be Christians at all. *That's only seven people for each true disciple!*

Seven people in ten years. With the church full of listeners, that sounds like blue sky. A mirage. But with the church full of communicators, it could be a slam dunk.

When my father was born in 1899, there were only ten Christian congregations worldwide for every people-group without a native gospel witness. By 1990, the ratio was 583 to one![46] That's progress any way you slice it!

Now, God plans to cross-pollinate the still-suffering church—from Bucharest to Beijing—with the rich and sophisticated western church... thus buttressing *them* and revitalizing *us!* That is His overall blueprint.

But do His plans always work out? Does God always win?

No. Thanks to His questionable taste in strategy (using human accomplices), He often loses, short term. It's kind of like letting your three-year-old help you hang wallpaper.

So in the '90s, we could lose some big battles. No one knows exactly how much mischief the Red and once-Red governments may yet do in this decade. But the God of History will *not* lose the Great War for Earth. He has exciting plans for the newly-free church *and* the church here in North America.

The New World Is Approaching

When the Western world first became systematically unified—under the bureaucratic oppression of Caesar Augustus—it was the tripwire for the First Advent.

Now we have a world on the brink of nobody knows what, with Communism nearing total collapse and the EC forming a whole new Europe. Surely their united Europe will not take long before it tries to become a grand Atlantic alliance with the U.S.... and then soon a world alliance, a "new world order."

Perhaps that alliance will be a tripwire for the Second Advent. Or perhaps that Advent will be delayed by the massive Christian bloodbath that may be required before the Crescent turns to the Cross. Or perhaps some further challenge awaits. Who knows?

But whatever comes to pass, the impending cyclone of events will not leave us the leisure to continue with closed churches. We *must* work toward Biblical patterns.

So as we sail into these uncharted seas, how greatly we need to be salt and light and to turn many to righteousness. How greatly we need to meet the Prince of Darkness with the *full force* of the entire church arrayed in a battle formation where each and every warrior knows his talents and tasks.

How greatly we need to make the lines of communication to God and each other open.

Now.

---

46. Statistics from the Center for World Mission.

Optional Reading
A. Back to the Future Church:
The One That Can Save the Many

We are rapidly moving into the fourth major era of Christianity.

With or without any slight help from this book, the church is now entering the open era, in which your jaded eyes will see things they have never seen before.

- You're going to see a closeness between God and His people that has not existed widely in 1700 years.
- You're going to see a bond of warmth and love between believers that was virtually impossible under the old system of staring at the pulpit in silence.
- You're going to see a flowering of laity-led ministries that will expand and transform the work of Christ on earth.

In bare outline, here is the church's past and future:

	The Early Church	The Catholic Era	The Protestant Era	The Open Church
Emphasis:	Commitment to One Another	The Sacraments	Preaching the Word	Participation
Problems:	Heresies, Persecution	Shallowness, Repression	Schisms, Bickering	(as yet unknown)
Strengths:	Growth, Holiness	Stability	Biblical Knowledge	Maturity, Outreach
Center of Authority:	Laymen	The Priest	The Pastor	Laymen
Main Meeting Activity:	Worship, Sharing	Worship	Easy Listening	Worship, Sharing

I apologize for such a simplistic table, but I want you to be wise to this one fact: The open church is not just the 957th technique for getting better results under the same old set of circumstances. It creates a whole new set of circumstances. Doctrine aside, it's more different from today's Protestant church than the Protestant church was from the Catholic.

This table may also remind you of another major point: that ideas have consequences. *The Early, the Catholic, and the Protestant churches all came with a new culture.* Realize that:

- The early believers erased (at least temporarily) the heathen gods and eased the extreme oppression of the individual.
- The explosion of the church after A.D. 313 created a truly catholic Catholic church—and a whole new society of faintly-Christianized, powerless serfs.
- The Protestant rebellion, along with its secular mirror image, the Renaissance, created a feisty new mindset that spawned the Industrial Revolution, the Enlightenment, the civil rights movement, adult-proof bottle caps, and numerous other cultural innovations.

Luther came along when the Renaissance was well under way. In like manner, the open church has come along just a few years after Mario Savio urged the dubious pioneers of the Free Speech Movement to "throw their bodies on the cogs and levers" of the impersonal institutionalism of Cal Berkeley, thus sparking a sub-culture of hippies that turned into yuppies and thence into a vast bloc of boomers who always insist, above all, upon being *heard and treated as individuals.*

The massive open church movement that I see swarming in from the horizon will not be led by people under 35. They're too busy taking sermon notes and filling up their minds with the framework of a godly worldview. They have yet to reach the point of disillusionment. They will eagerly join the movement in droves, but not in the vanguard.

Instead, the leaders of the open church movement will be men and women 35 to 75 who:

- are bored silly with the repetitiveness and anonymity of the church's closed services
- are soul-weary of sitting on a spiritual plateau and walking a treadmill of activities
- are experienced enough to know they're being shortchanged.

Why the Church Will Open

1. God wants it.

Just before he was crucified, the Lord Jesus prayed for his disciples,

Holy Father, protect them by the power of your name—the name you gave me—so that they may be one as we are one....

[But] My prayer is not for them alone. I pray also for those who will believe in me through their message, that all of them may be one, Father, just as you are in me and I am in you. May they also be in us so that the world may believe that you have sent me. I have given them the glory that you gave me, that they may be one as we are one: I in them and you in me. May they be brought to complete unity to let the world know that you sent me and have loved them even as you have loved me. (John 17, *NIV*, emphasis added)

As you know, oneness doesn't come from sitting in the same pew or singing the same songs or even agreeing on the same theology. Nor does it come from the warm sort of camaraderie you get from joining a Greek college fraternity and having a beer bust with your "brothers."

Oneness comes from how you *function* as part of the group. If you work together well, you're a team. A unity. A *one*.

If not, you're an association. A collection of parts. Perhaps even a typical church.

Look at the words I've underlined above. God doesn't just want us to be "of a like mind." He wants us to be of the *same* mind. As He is. And you don't get that kind of unity in an audience, even if they've all signed the same 20-page doctrinal statement.

Long term, the open church is not a luxury. It's what God has been trying to bring back for 1700 long years: a living, functioning unity—the bride of Christ, laboriously collected out of the junkyard of humanity; a muddy, chaotic diversity blended through heart-to-heart interaction into a pure and whole living body.

2. Christians will demand it.

The natives are restless tonight.

Most anywhere you go, you can hear mumblings of discontent. And when you don't hear any, you can ask a few semi-innocent, leading questions, and *presto*—instant discontent! It's right there beneath the surface—unspoken, unarticulated, but very real. Just ask your Christian friends:

- Over the years, have you kept growing spiritually, or do you spend most of your time on plateaus?
- Is Sunday morning worship a stretching and growing experience for you?
- Does your church work as a team when they get together?
- Would you like to be free to exercise the gifts God has given you among the brothers and sisters?
- Do you truly feel shepherded and cared for at church?

Keep asking these kinds of questions, and you'll get some replies like, "What color is the sky on the planet where you live?" I estimate that over eighty per cent of U.S. evangelicals, charismatics, and fundamentalists have strong sympathies for bringing back the open church right now, today. (That doesn't mean they would agree with everything in this book, of course.)

One of the great strengths of the closed church is order. We now have nearly 100% order and control. Once you get everybody trained to file in, sit silently, and file out, maintaining order is a snap.

But in an open church, people's yearning to be free, to grow daily, and to exercise their true potential produces a constant need to maintain order. Lack of order was an awful problem at Corinth, and it can occasionally be a *brief* problem today. But it's worth the vigilance. The only unity worth a half-hearted hoot is the kind that comes through *individual freedom in harmony with group order.* Do you see? When there's no freedom to do or say anything, keeping order is duck soup. And without the freedom to function, there's no functional unity, only mental unity.

3. The world needs it.

Get a firm grip on these pages. This next point is tough, but well worth your attention.

The world has a very big problem: It doesn't know how to get along with itself. It has never reconciled the needs of the individual with the needs of the group. Either the group dominates the individual, or it's dog eat dog.

On a national scale, it's dictatorship or anarchy. In chaotic countries like India, nothing much gets done unless you "know someone." In countries like China, the individual gets strangled by the central octopus.

The motto of the United States is *E Pluribus Unum*, "One Out of Many." Along with our religious faith, it is—or was—our main strength.

Neither the U.S. nor the world, however, has ever quite grasped this principle. Unity has fought diversity throughout the ages. When unity won, all particulars, divisions, and individuality were swallowed up by the whole, the static *one*, and people were dominated by statism. When diversity won, the world shattered into unrelated forces, the universe became a multiverse, and anarchy reigned.

- The Tower of Babel was the classic statement of individuals seeking to make themselves both one and divine. It quickly dissolved in chaos.
- In Egypt, "the state was not one institution among many but rather the essence of divine order for life and the means of communication between heaven, earth, and hell. Life therefore was totally and inescapably statist."[47] The pyramids are the ultimate symbol of that.
- Throughout the early history of Mesopotamia, anarchy was the constant threat. Before Alexander the Great and the Romans arrived, the area was a battlefield for the Sumerians and Akkadians, the Assyrians and Babylonians.
- The Greeks never unified beyond the city-state stage. Not coincidentally, their philosophy never progressed beyond a stalemated tension between form (ideas) and matter, a dualism of the static *one* (taught by Parmenides) vs. the chaotic *many* (taught by Heraclitus).
- The Roman Empire grew stagnant, and the worship of the emperor,

---

47. R.J. Rushdoony, <u>The One and The Many</u>, p.44

halfhearted at best, withered into lethargy and cynicism as men sought a semblance of regeneration through chaos festivals and orgies.

When Jesus Christ appeared and established the church, the foundation was laid down clearly in Scripture for a solution to the problems of the one vs. the many. Unfortunately, the church leaders had their hands full sorting out the long initial string of heresies; and the laity, having been nicely redeployed throughout the Roman Empire in A.D. 70 by Titus, were busy adjusting to—and converting—their pagan neighbors.

The prevailing philosophy of the middle ages was scholasticism. Predictably, it gave birth to two main schools of thought: realism, in which all things are basically *one*, and nominalism, in which all things are basically *many*. No solution there. So the battle goes on today:

- Families fly apart by the tens of millions. It's Mom vs. Dad vs. Junior vs. Sis. We can't keep them together any more.
- Overnight the USSR flip-flops from tyranny to civil wars and breakdown.
- The Democrats fight the Republicans tooth and nail. Common ground has vanished.
- The America-First crowd battles the trendier forces of "cultural pluralism." No one's going to win that one.
- In fact, it's war everywhere:
    —students vs. their universities
    —Iraq vs. the world
    —companies vs. their employees
    —the middle class vs. the lower class
    —the rich vs. everybody
    —Congress vs. the states
    —states vs. cities
    —depositors vs. S&Ls
    —businessmen vs. OSHA
    —doctors vs. the FDA
    —pro-lifers vs. pro-choicers
    —the media vs. everybody
    —minorities vs. majorities
    ...and everybody's suing the pants off everyone else.

The one vs. the many. Unity vs. diversity. How can the world satisfy the needs of both? *Apart from Christians, it can't.* It has no model to copy.

The only known grouping of persons that works closely in perfect harmony is the Holy Trinity. The Father, Son, and Holy Spirit are the only example or paradigm that allows us to envision a unitary thing with intelligent parts that don't conflict. God is the only known entity that is both one and "many."

Without the example of the Godhead, the world's people will never understand how the universe is meant to function. All their systems will have order without freedom or freedom without order.

The Christian Solution (And It's Not Democracy)

Our current idol is voting. Nearly all Christians believe in it. But democracy is no cure-all. Voting is just a non-violent way to defeat those you're opposed to and force them to do your will.

Churches that rely on voting do recognize the worth of each believer, and that's good. But a pure reliance on voting disregards all of our unique characteristics, our very *unequal* God-given abilities to contribute to a body-life solution that will help the whole assembly. Voting divides us into camps, whereas supportive fellowship and prayer unites us.

The typical democratic country eventually generates millions of contentious, me-first citizens who achieve *barely* enough agreement to stave off chaos. Without heavy influence by the church, democracies have always been short-lived balancing acts that last about two centuries and then fragment.

Democracy was never noted as a perfect way to blend the many into a happy *one*. It has largely been a device to "turn the rascals out" and bring in a new set of rascals. It's too inefficient to be anywhere near ideal. Churchill even called it "the worst form of government except all those other forms that have been tried from time to time." It gives us just enough freedom to drive our elected leaders crazy. As Charles de Gaulle once lamented, "How can you govern a country with two hundred forty-six varieties of cheese?"

Now, after 1700 years, the church is once again in a position to cure the world's chronic conflict between the one and the many, freedom and order, Cheddar and mozzarella. How? Mostly by proclaiming the Trinity and mirroring It visibly, in an earthly pattern. Here is the #1 Bible clue to how we can do it:

> *And we all, with unveiled faces, beholding [reflecting, mir-roring, contemplating] the glory of the Lord, are being changed into His likeness, from one degree of glory to the next.*

(II Corinthians 3:18, a key verse to memorize)

As we behold and mirror God in pure worship, we will be changed by degrees into a visible and copyable model of His love, strength, wisdom—and harmony. ("That they may be one as we are one.") **The world will never really understand the Godhead, but it can easily see the strange unity of our motley team of Christians who truly love each other and "esteem the others better than themselves."**[48]

---

48. Democracy delivers a fragile unity based on self-interest, if not downright selfishness. Of course, self-interest is quite legitimate; Old Testament law endorses it in hundreds of ways. But Christianity can now deliver a better unity based upon *loving, considerate interaction.* Whereas the world's unity is strained by diversity, our unity is a product of our diversity.

A bonus thought: I personally feel that the church can be not only a *model* of salvation but a *means* of salvation. Once we learn to tap our supernatural ability to unite for action, we can be a truly effective influence for good, transforming the world from top to bottom.

But my publisher reminds me that this is a book about the church, not culture or politics, so for now, I'll desist. In the long run, however, I know that God's power can save the world's peoples from catastrophic ruin, and I fully expect that a free, open church will soon respond to the Lord's leading and use this power, not in order to be a ruling bloc, but to be a respect bloc, a strong salt-and-light influence for righteousness.

B. Plug into Excitement!

God is doing so much today it makes me woozy. And if you subscribe to as many publications as I do, you're woozy, too—with excitement. You can't go through your daily mail without stopping to readjust your brain to the world *du jour.*

The institutional church has no way to tell the man in the pew about any of it. Most of what gets to him funnels through the pastor—a narrow funnel indeed when you consider the vast amount of news that players need to know today.

Here's a much-needed solution, one that will add more new activity to your church than you'll know what to do with: Allow a few of your reader types (men and women) to form a *Global Intelligence Team* (GIT) and cover such areas as:

- new acts and movements of God
- new books on diverse topics
- mobilization opportunities
- your adopted sister churches overseas
- missions
- world events affecting missions
- opportunities to write letters about pending legislation

Just as your worship and body life sessions will enable each member to feel a part of your particular congregation, so *the work of a GIT will enable each member to feel a part of the church universal, which is a different but exciting feeling.*

The Western news media have turned almost everyone into ignoramuses by their extremely spotty, biased, and secular coverage, and if your members don't get any wider input than most, they have only a sketchy picture of the world.

They can't affect events they don't know of. So in time, they can turn into spiritual provincials who understand little except their own back yards. How can they pray about something they haven't heard of? Or write letters of support? Or send missionaries. Or go?

Do they know about the Dinkas in Sudan? The National Institute for Reconciliation in South Africa? The 325,800 Christians martyred in an average year? They're probably well-posted on the concerns of your own missionaries, but there are another five billion people out there.

The GIT should be given authority and responsibility to gather the broadest possible range of useful information and present it to the church. Their output may be given during the Sunday service or another service or even in print (perhaps via desktop publishing).

Four or five eager beavers doing steady research can create for your congregation a vast panorama of spiritual adventures as far as the eye can see. Every member will be tempted to explore it in depth. Every member will be enriched. And your pastor won't have to plow through fifteen publications in a vain effort to keep up with what's going on.

Besides, this will help to keep your eggheads (always chronic malcontents) out of mischief.

C. Tips on Meetings

There is always more to learn about life in the community of the saints! Here are a few more helps for you, collected with considerable help from Gene Edwards. His *How to Meet* (see bibliography) will explain these concepts further for you.

1. Ever wished you could take an advance peek into heaven?

The heavenly scenes in Revelation 4 and 5 will give you some idea of what it's like and how infinitely rich an experience it will be to stand in God's presence.

But right here on earth, you can have some of the same breath-stealing experiences in your open meetings with God. *The possibilities for what you can do are almost infinite because God Himself is infinite, and He can be approached in an infinite number of ways. You and your fellow disciples will spend the rest of eternity exploring the endless dimensions of worship and sharing. In other words, **there's no end to the great and wonderful things you can do in a true, open community of believers ... starting now.***

Therefore, enrich your meetings with a broad range of activities. There is a universal human tendency to settle into a rut, doing the same **types** of things month after month. Whether it's worship and praise or fellowship and sharing, your meetings can easily drift into a sameness of form. You can add a great deal of depth by showing people how to inject a variety of contributions:

- Encourage!
- Exhort!
- Admonish!

- Read Scripture aloud—normally with an explanation of why you're reading it (don't make them guess!)
- Pray (being sure to include, over the months, all types and topics of prayer: individual, group, praise/worship, petition, intercession, repentance, sentence prayers, conversational prayer, and lots of thanksgiving).
- Testify! Give a report of God's grace in your life recently.
- Recount a story of something you saw or heard or experienced, a story that teaches a spiritual truth or a fact about God.
- Prophesy (unless you're in a denomination that doesn't believe in prophecy, in which case you can probably still get away with it, but you'll have to call it something else). Prophecy is, at root, an especially acute insight into the mind of God on some subject or event. It doesn't *have* to involve predictions.
- Meditate/Reflect on what the last person just said.
- Preach! It doesn't have to be a full-course sermon. Three minutes will do just fine. Even two is OK; you have to start somewhere.
- Repent and confess. If you get a strong confirmation of forgiveness from the brothers and sisters in the meeting, it will give you much reassurance of God's forgiveness.
- Reinforce! When someone says something that resonates with your spirit, back him or her up with a brief response, a word of agreement, or even an elaboration of the point. He or she will love you for it, and you'll build unity that will last like the pyramids.
- Take notes!
- Get physical! Don't go way beyond the norm for your group and embarrass people, but loosen up and diversify occasionally into the physical dimension. Try things like kneeling, holding hands to pray, laying on hands if someone needs extra-special prayer, or even dancing (but not on the ceiling, please).
- Lead a song, a hymn, a round, a chorus—or divide up the assembly and sing antiphonal songs (men/women, left/right side, adults/kids, Republicans/Democrats, etc.)
- Sing a song yourself—or devise a duet, trio, etc.
- And if you're not up to any of the above, *ask for help!*

2. Stamp out spectating!

New Testament churches were led strictly by laymen, not by pastors. The common folk took care of their own meetings (and baptisms and weddings and Communions and everything else).

If you think you could *never* feel comfortable conducting a baptism or the Lord's Supper, then you have been truly wounded by today's closed system. The Reformation doctrine of "the priesthood of the believer" means, in the end, that you are as deserving and worthy to be a priest as any human on this planet. Your status as a "layperson" puts *no* limits on you. Rejoice!

In the early days, there was no pre-set order of worship. Contributions were mostly spontaneous, as the Spirit led. In a typical congregation, there was no single person who always spoke. "Speakers" were itinerant and fairly rare.

On the other hand, there were no pure spectators, either. Everyone was expected to take part. Shyness was accepted, silence wasn't.

Preaching and sharing of wisdom was briefer in those days, of course. Today's feature-length sermons tend to squelch shorter contributions, the sort of contributions an ordinary rustic believer could have managed in the early days. That's why the modern-day sermon really didn't appear on the face of the earth until the Fourth Century, when the influence of pagan Greek orators brought it in.[49] And the idea of a sermon being brought **every** Sunday by the **same person** (while everyone else sat silently) was still 1400 years away! The pastoral concept as we know it was also 1400 years away— in a different world.

But the practice of dividing up Christians between clergy and laity erupted within 300 years. That was when Constantine came along and spread it across the Empire. All the freedoms and practices of the early Christians evaporated as if they had never existed. By A.D. 500, the image of a joyful early church seemed as antique and foreign as it does to us today. The idea that *you* are the meeting, no clergy need be present, and no elders or deacons need to watchdog the meeting was lost like sunken treasure in a storm upon the high seas.

Friend, until you've been in a red-hot meeting where everyone's life is being changed and there is **no** human leadership present, you simply haven't tasted one of the greatest pleasures of the Christian life: being part of the true **body** of Christ. To you, that treasure still lies buried on the ocean floor.

3. Break the news properly.

When your pastor announces the initial open meeting(s), he should take a series of sermons to carefully explain the advantages and benefits of the open church for the individual. He should also make sure everyone understands this is a return to the tried and true Biblical pattern rather than some far-out experiment "to see if it will work."

In his sermons, he must prepare people's hearts as well as their minds. Some important truths he will probably include are:

a. *The huge difference between "coming to get fed" and "coming to take part."*

---

49. The modern American sermon was not known in the First Century. Messages, yes; sermons, no. The sermon is about the only remaining form of communication in this culture where it's not proper to answer back!

You'll notice in the Gospels that time and again, Jesus started a speech but wound up in a dialogue. I suspect that even the Sermon on the Mount served as an introduction to many a question and comment from the audience (Matthew 5:2).

b. *The need to bear one another's burdens.* The typical attitude of "you mind your business and I'll mind mine" must be replaced with an understanding that we must now start being committed to helping each other like a true Christian family.
c. *The need to bring something to share in an open meeting.* They've never had to do this before! In the traditional closed meeting, you can come for years with empty hands, empty head, and empty heart—and no one will be the wiser. But in an open meeting, you're the show!
d. *Tips on taking part.* The basic logic and mechanics of an open meeting.
e. *The priesthood of the believer.* The "Miranda" sermon, where he "reads you your rights"!

4. Do your PR. Have the courtesy to inform everyone about what's happening! Depending on how many inactives you have on your church mailing list, you may want to mail out to everyone an announcement of the coming changes. To add impact and persuasion to the mailing, you may want to insert a copy of *There's a New Church Coming*, available in printed or photocopiable form. This is a little folder that tells the benefits of the open church and gives suggestions on how best to take part in it. (See the bibliography.)

5. Keep everyone on the Q.T. Make sure people understand they're now expected to meet with God during the week, and that their Quiet Time with Him is always going to be the wellspring and mainstay of what they bring to the meeting. *Failure to do this is the #1 cause of the demise of open meetings.*

Whether it's a prayer, exhortation, psalm, hymn, confession, or whatever, it comes from God. Whether it springs from circumstances or reading a book or anything else, it still comes from God, who is the author and center of an open meeting of His saints.

6. Get a little commitment to care for one another.

If everybody's into the open church just for what he can get out of it, it will fizzle and fade. Believe me, if you ever face rough times, the **only** two things that will get you through are the blood of Christ and a proactive love for each other. I could go on for pages, but trust me, this is a basic requirement.

7. Don't expect miracles. Nothing is automatic in an open church.

You are the show, trouper. You can't just sit. If no one contributes anything worthwhile, the service is over. Fini. Kaput. If you're going to sit around like at a wake, you might as well kick off your shoes, lie down in the pew, and take a nap while you wait for the next snowfall to come and cover you up.

After years of frustration and being forbidden to take an active part in a meeting of believers, your mind can start to create a great romantic fallacy: that the moment the lid comes off, everyone will jump to his feet and eloquently pour forth the suppressed yearnings and Socratic thoughts of a lifetime. And every contribution will, of course, blend seamlessly with those coming before and after.

Well, roughly half the time, you do get a non-stop string of heartfelt contributions, and everybody leaves the meeting with a lump in his throat or a hanky in her hand. And the chain-reaction sharing and worship and ministry may go on for weeks and weeks. But I can almost promise you two challenges:

    a. It won't be seamless right from the git-go. You'll have herky-jerky contributions, sporadic singing, desultory prayers, lumpy pauses, uneven exhortations, intermittent sharing ... and gobs of semi-garbled, joyful, uplifting, happy exclamations from nervous-but-delighted spiritual toddlers taking their first steps in public. Plus a few awful contributions. *Count on it.*

    b. No matter how good it is at the start, it may not last long without some help. The initial exhuberance usually yields to the reality of a need to refuel. *Sooner or later, your people will have to learn to **prepare** for the meeting and consciously bring some new thing to it.*

8. Get thee to the church on time.

If you dribble in and start in a weak, rambling way, you can wave bye-bye to body life. With no prearranged order of the meeting and no one leading, dribbling in is death-wish behavior.

In a closed church, you can read the bulletin and see what you've missed. But come late to an open meeting, and what can you do? Dive right in and hope that you're in tune with things? Or just sit there until you think you've figured out where everybody's coming from today?

Not a happy choice. And nine times out of ten, when you start weak, you end weak.

Plus, the prompt ones who begin on time with a fraction of the eventual participants will usually feel kind of demoralized right from the start.

9. Come to build up the other guy or gal. Rise above small talk, especially casual talk about your friends. Come to the table to meet the Lord and each other in a brand new way.

10. Learn better ways to pray.

The style of prayer we Christians use in groups is *abominable*.

By default, by our total lack of thinking and innovation, we have remained mired in "oratorical prayer" for perhaps 17 or 18 centuries. Our long-winded, non-interactive kind of prayer is **incredibly** intimidating to new people, and *quite* intimidating to over half of the rest of us! Why do we do this to ourselves—and to God?

In the open church of the future, we must bring in a new standard for our group praying: *easy and inviting.* I'll mention two types:

   a. Sentence prayers. (Very easy to learn.) In a <u>true</u> sentence-prayer period, no one gets more than one sentence (with a maximum of one semicolon)! This, of course, makes it quite difficult to start <u>and</u> finish a topic of any complexity at all, and thus the participants are thrust into a delightful dependency upon one another. If the other guy can only *introduce* a subject, then *you* must be alert and supportive enough to pick up his ball and run with it.

     Likewise, you'll discover how enormously encouraging it can be when you "toss out" a burden of yours with one sentence, then sit back and enjoy listening while half a dozen other people jump on it and get involved in lifting up the subject to God. This experience is about the opposite of the usual pattern where you pour out an elaborate, difficult prayer, and all you get in the way of response is a scattering of mumbled, sickly "amens."

   b. Conversational prayer. This is the most advanced, mature form of group prayer. It's more difficult to learn than sentence prayers, but allows a more natural sort of interaction, and each individual contribution can have more depth of thought and feeling. If you have a dead serious team of players who truly want to change the world, you could profit from having one of them "specialize" in the techniques and literature of prayer. The classic book on this is the very practical and helpful best-seller *Prayer: Conversing with God* by my friend Rosalind Rinker. (See the bibliography.)

11. There *are* things that can spoil an open fellowship meal, of course, and I suppose I should mention the main one: asking questions and wanting explanations of nearly every comment made.

It's really a dumb thing to do. But even worse is the fact that there's always some compliant soul sitting there who is dumb enough to try to answer every last one of those out-of-order questions! A matched pair of these detour darlings can make a whole supper celebration go sour. You can easily find yourself not worshipping and fellowshipping about the Lord, but dealing with something that is purely intellectual and doctrinal, full of all sorts of knowledge and philosophy and even dispute. (In case of a dispute, your stomach itself will tell you something's wrong!)

12. Keep moving ahead.

Avoid dead silences—the kind with uneasy restlessness. When the silence gets three feet thick and you'd need an 800-ton icebreaker ship to break through it, you're dead in the water.

Your team must <u>never</u> let this happen.

Sure, silence can be good. For instance, if someone says something that leaves everyone stunned or choked up or awed or just needing a little time to absorb it all, you *need* some silence.

The kind of silence I'm denouncing is what they call in radio, "dead air time," a silence that doesn't belong there. Dead silence can flatten a meeting like a steam roller going over a box of marshmallows.

Believe me, there's no mystery about why dead silences appear. It's because your leadership kicked back and didn't lead. (*Leaderless* does not mean *leadershipless*.) It's because *you* didn't prepare for the meeting. It's because *no one* has anything to contribute.

As the saying goes, "You can't beat something with nothing." And in this case, you can't beat a traditional service, where the pastor sweats for five or ten hours preparing a great sermon, with an open service where nobody prepares anything.

Take a warning from the Quaker "silent meetings," which are pretty much dead these days. Originally, they were full of testimonies, song, and sharing. But the silent spots crept in, grew like a cancer, and ate away the life of the meeting.

13. Let Christ express Himself at your meetings.

In the long run, there's only one way you'll ever function as the body of Christ: *Make Christ the head of your meeting.*

If the man on the platform is being a mouth, everyone else has to be an ear. But if the Spirit of Christ is the head, he can activate a finger here, an arm there, then an eye or two and a few toes—all in good order.

When you have forty brothers and sisters singing a hymn, and you listen very, very carefully, you'll hear a forty-first voice. It is none other than the Lord Jesus Christ himself, living out his desires and fulfilling the wishes of the Father here on earth, right in your meeting.

In Genesis, it is plainly stated that man is created to bear the image of God and subdue the earth. Now, if a single believer is a living image of the Most High God, just imagine how much more dazzling an image it is when a dozen or several hundred believers incorporate the image of God in a far more detailed and complete way!!

But alas, for 1700 years we haven't seen many groups of believers banding together in a body with any kind of true body life, where arms and legs and hands can function as God intended. What we've seen is a lot of individuals looking like the meat counter at Safeway, where you see chicken parts laid out in rows: a package of thighs, a package of necks, a package of legs ... and none of it gives you any idea whatsoever of how a real, live chicken looks and moves.

Christ wants a place where He is head. He has given us elders to lead us in matters outside the meeting. But when the church gathers, there is to be *no covering over the head of Jesus Christ.* He is to be the head of the meeting.

When you come into a meeting, you must turn to your spirit with no foolishness and keep your full attention on the Lord. We are the body, Christ is the head. If the members can't act as a body in an open meeting, then what you get is a Corinthian free-for-all, a random mass of body parts acting on their own, either glorifying themselves, fighting the other parts, or simply doing nothing and dying a slow death of the spirit.

If a body can't function, it means death. That's why it usually takes only about two years in a closed church for a newborn Christian to stop growing, plateau, stagnate, and lose any possibility of growing into a towering spiritual presence in the world. Lions don't grow in small cages.

D. Why Real Men Don't Play Church

The church of the Almighty God has a chronic shortage of mighty men.

If you haven't noticed that yet, you've been inhaling too many gas fumes on the freeway.

For 1700 years, the church has catered to harmless souls who wouldn't rock a rowboat. Consider this true anecdote from *The Joyful Noiseletter:*

The Rev. Gary Schindler is a rector at two Episcopal churches in Pennsylvania.

After the first service at St. Martin's, he has to rush to the second service at St. George's—often a bit late. But the St. George's parking lot is always full, and he used to wind up parking down the street and trotting to the church in full ecclesiastical garb.

The senior warden tried to solve the problem by putting up a sign saying "Reserved for Rector." Success was spotty. So the warden added a second sign:

YOU PARK,
YOU PREACH.

No one has parked there since!

Sure, that's funny. Why? Because, supposedly, no layman in his right mind would welcome the scary fate of being thrust before the entire congregation and told to give the sermon!

Think for a moment about the broad sexual connotations of standing up and speaking and leading the church. Is that the sort of thing you'd associate more with masculinity or femininity?

Then think about the connotations of sitting, listening passively, and being led. Is that more compatible with maleness or femaleness? There, in a nutshell, is why today's church attracts more women than men.

Women don't feel a need to prove their womanhood. Men, on the other hand, have an astonishing psychospiritual need to prove their manhood over and over and over. And sitting in rows doesn't do it.

Paul comments that "it is *disgraceful* for a woman to speak in the church" and to teach men. I suspect the main reason he was so extreme on that point is that it kind of puts men in the posture of women. Tragically, we today have put men in the posture of women—not by placing women over them, but by placing **other men** over them in debilitating ways. With the same net effect!

Christian men have a general reputation as being less like John Wayne and more like good ol' Charlie Brown. That's why millions of single Christian women would kill rhinoceroses with their bare hands to find what they call a **"real man."** *You don't produce "real men" by making them sit in rows and listen for seventy years. You do it by making them stand up and boldly proclaim what's in their hearts and in the Word.*

What you had in the fourth century was *the feminization of the church.* It became more suitable for women than for men. Before that time, men had somewhere to go. Up. With the constant splitting into more and more house churches, leadership needs were heavy and participation was mandatory. Also, persecution flushed out the invertebrates.

Today, there just aren't nearly enough available men. You probably know that already. It's tempting to look around in churches in upscale suburbia, where traditional families still abound, and conclude that the male-female imbalance is not too serious. But it is. And still the problem is ignored.

Ask any woman. Men are so underrepresented on church rolls that millions of young women, seeing their marriage chances diminishing, have reprioritized their lives, married marginal believers, and dropped out of sight. If they hadn't, our female-male ratio would be even worse.

The only solution is to bring back the open church. Let men be men again.

Lions hate cages. Prepare a place and an orbit for the young lions and paladins of today. Give them a chance, in the midst of the congregation of the faithful, to act, to speak, to do, to lead.

Let them grow bold in steps of faith by. . .
* speaking with heart and mind in your sharing time
* calling down the shekinah glory of God's presence into your worship time
* giving a short meditation from the pulpit as a warmup to your minister's sermon
* preaching a ten-minute sermonette on a passage of Scripture or a common problem in life
* calling for several others to join in a team project
* calling for the whole congregation to take some personal step of faith, to repent of some sin, to accept a new challenge from God
* in time, even leading in the creation of a daughter church.

Is all this too much to expect?

Not at all. Lions will accept no less.

Contributors

Tommy Barnett has been the senior pastor of Phoenix First Assembly of God in Arizona since 1978. Known as one of America's leading churchmen, his annual pastor's conferences and athlete's conventions have drawn thousands from around the world.

Gene Edwards is a retired Southern Baptist minister who served as a pastor and evangelist before entering upon a global 25-year ministry on the deeper Christian life. He is the author of twelve books and one of the leading figures in the house church movement. He and his wife, Helen, live in New England.

Leo Godzich is pastor of special projects at Phoenix First Assembly of God church in Arizona. Formerly an award-winning journalist and soccer player, he has written more than 300 articles in various journals and magazines. He is founder and director of LAMP Ministries, an AIDS outreach, and chairman of Kids First, a coalition of groups involved in political matters on children.

Jim Hayford, Sr., is pastor of the First Foursquare Church in Santa Barbara, California. He is a noted authority in church planting, and his new book, *Contending for the Authentic,* describes how a New Testament church can be established in today's society. He planted a church in Danville, California, that grew to 2,000 in 12 years while planting fifteen daughter churches.

Tom Mohn is two-thirds of the 1½ full time workers with Bread of Life Ministries in Tulsa, Oklahoma. He is widely recognized as the former announcer for Oral Roberts and a seminar leader in his own right.

Dr. Ray C. Stedman was long known as one of the most prominent pastors on the West Coast. He was the founding pastor of Peninsula Bible Church in Redwood City, California, and wrote the classic *Body Life, From Guilt to Glory,* and *Talking to My Father.*

Good Reading

Some of these books are only available through the publisher or a particular ministry. In each case, we list the address.

Alvin, Joe *The Lost Sacrament: The Way To Serve Your Fellow-Man Through The Use Of Your Talents.* Good book on the use of spiritual gifts in serving others. Charis Publications P.O. Box 506, La Puente, CA 91747 (1978) 80pp.

Bercot, David W. *Common Sense: A New Approach to Understanding Scripture.* An excellent book on understanding how Scripture is interpreted, with a clear and simple approach. There are many stories and illustrations. This is a great companion to his other book in this bibliography. Scroll Publishing, Tyler, TX 75711 (1992) 173 pp.

Bercot, David W. *Will The Real Heretics Please Stand Up.* Perhaps the best book in this list. The style is easy to read and informative. The book doesn't really offer solutions, but points out what many of the problems are and leads readers to think for themselves. There is a ton of information as to where our church traditions come from. No matter what denomination you ascribe allegiance to, you will find some of yourself in this book. Necessary reading. Your friendly Christian bookstore can order this for you, or it's available from the publisher. Scroll Publishing Co., Tyler, TX 75706 (1989)

Banks, Robert *Paul's Idea of Community.* A book about the freedom of Christians and the early house churches in their historical setting. William B. Eerdmans Publishing Company, Grand Rapids, Michigan (1988) 208pp.

Banks, Robert & Julia *The Church Comes Home.* A model to assist all denominations in bringing the church home. Good side reading to *The Open Church.* Albatross Books, P.O. Box 131, Claremont, CA 91711 (1986) 261pp

Berguson, Johnny and Juanita *What Ever Happened To Christianity?: A Loving Challenge to Current Church Structure.* Reads like a good background briefing to go along with *The Open Church,* with special emphasis on relationships within the body of believers. Available from Kingdom Co., U.S. Route 6 East, P.O. Box 506, Mansfield, PA 16933 $2.00 plus $1.00 shipping.

Crabtree, Davida Foy *The Empowering Church: How One Congregation Supports Lay People's Ministries in the World.* A mainline Protestant pastor discusses her experience with lay ministries. Available from Alban Institute, 4125 Nebraska Ave. NW, Washington, DC 20016 72pp.

Edwards, Gene *Avoiding a Church Split.* The title says it all. Available from The SeedSowers, P.O. Box 3568, Beaumont, TX, 77704. (409) 838-3774. $6.95 plus $1.00 shipping.

Edwards, Gene *How To Meet.* This book is the only one in its field! Tells you how and what to do in an open meeting. A wealth of down-to-earth, practical information. It is published as a three-ring binder, and has room for notes and additions. Available from The SeedSowers, P.O. Box 3568, Beaumont, TX 77704 (409) 838-3774 $9.95 plus $1.00 shipping.

04212. (207) 795-6615 $9.95 plus $1.00 shipping. (Available November, 1992)

Edwards, Gene *Letters to a Devastated Christian.* A series of letters to someone coming out of an oppressive, authoritarian church. Tyndale House Publishers.

Edwards, Gene *The Revolution. Volume One: The Story of the Early Church, A.D.30-47.* The exhilarating story of the Jerusalem Christians and their spread to Antioch. The 4-volume work, when completed, will mark the first time the complete story of the first-century believers has ever been chronicled. Breathtaking glimpses and drama unfold on every page. Available from The SeedSowers, P.O. Box 3568, Beaumont, TX, 77704 (409) 838-3774 $7.95, plus $1.00 shipping.

Freeman, Hobart E. *Charismatic Body Ministry.* Good side reading about ministry in the body. Faith Publications P.O. Box 1156, Warsaw, Indiana 46580 78pp.

Galloway, Dale E. *20/20 Vision.* How to create a successful church with lay pastors and cell groups. Scott Publishing Company, 11731 S.E. Stevens Rd., Portland, OR 97266 (1986) 160pp.

George, Carl F. *Prepare Your Church for the Future.* The ultimate book on how to make changes in a church. Lavishly praised by the top leaders in church growth. Fleming H. Revell $10.95 (1991) 240pp.

Hughes, Richard T. *The American Quest for the Primitive Church.* Textbook style history, but excellent information. University of Illinois Press (1988) 257pp.

Kennedy, John W. *The Torch of the Testimony.* The story of believers outside of the mainstream church from A.D.300-1900. Available from The SeedSowers, P.O. Box 3568, Beaumont, TX, 77704. (409) 838-3774. $8.95, plus $1.00 shipping.

Kingdom Publishing "The Traditions of Men in the Churches of Men." Excellent booklet on the origins of church traditions. Kingdom Publishing, P.O. Box 68309, Indianapolis, IN 46268 (1989) 19pp.

Kingdom Publishing *Meetings In His Kingdom.* Good book on the format of different types of meetings and how to let God run the meetings. Kingdom Publishing, P.O. Box 68309, Indianapolis, IN 46268 (1990) 199pp.

Kingdom Publishing "Church Restoration: The Missing Link." Good booklet on restoring the church. Kingdom Publishing, P.O. Box 68309, Indianapolis, IN 46268 (1990) 11pp.

Liesch, Barry *People In The Presence of God.* Offers a Biblical perspective on the different models of worship and helps readers return to true worship. Probably the best book around on music in worship. Zondervan Publishing House (1988) 352pp.

Lockerbie, D. Bruce *Thinking And Acting Like A Christian.* Targets the personal lives of Christians in facilitating change and growth that affects home, church, work and leisure. Multnomah Press (1989) 172pp.

MacNair, Donald J. *The Living Church.* Teaches church leaders what the church as established by Christ ought to be. Great Commission Publications, 7401 Old York Road, Philadelphia, PA 19126 (1980) 167pp.

Mitchell, John G. *Fellowship.* A devotional study of the Epistles of John as they relate to the believers' relationships with others, particularly other Christians. Multnomah Press (1974) 189pp.

Moltmann, Jurgen *The Open Church: Invitation to Messianic Lifestyle.* No connection to this book. Some good points. By a german neo-orthodix German theologian. Fortunately a book on ecclesiology does not depend too much on theology. SCM Press LTD., London (1983)

Neighbour, Ralph W. *Where Do We Go From Here?* A guidebook for the Cell Group Church. Some of his ideas are useful for the open church. The book is filled with excellent explanations, charts and diagrams, and is written in a readable format. A good book to start with as a jumping-off platform. Available from the publisher. Touch Outreach Ministries, P.O. Box 19888, Houston, TX 77224. (800) 735-5865. $14.95, plus $2.00 shipping charge (1990) 400 pp.

Ogden, Greg *The New Reformation: Returning the Ministry to the People of God.* A more scholarly approach to the same ideas presented in *The Open Church.* Calvin and his works are quoted more frequently than Luther, but the primary suppositions are the same. Zondervan Publishing House, Grand Rapids, MI (1990) 224 pp.

Richards, Lawrence O. & Hoeldtke, Clyde *Church Leadership.* A textbook style presentation of the church as a living organism, with diagrams and charts presenting many aspects of the church and its leadership. Zondervan Publishing House, Grand Rapids (1980) 425pp.

Rinker, Rosalind *Learning Conversational Prayer.* A recent book, short (46 pages) and easy to read. Useful for helping people learn how to pray in a group Available in Catholic bookstores and from the publisher: Liturgical Press, Collegeville, MN $3.95 (1992)

Rinker, Rosalind *Prayer—Conversing with God.* The classic book on praying in a natural style. Zondervan (1987) $5.99. 128 pp.

Rutz, James *Better Than Church.* A slight adaptation of Part I of *The Open Church* for those involved in house churches. Available from The SeedSowers, P.O. Box 3568, Beaumont, TX, 77704 (409) 838-3774 $5.95, plus $1.00 shipping. 43pp.

Rutz, James "The Rebirth of the Church" Comprises mainly Part I of *The Open Church.* A packet of ten copies from The SeedSowers is $9.00 plus $1.00 shipping. P.O. Box 3568, Beaumont, TX, 77704 (409) 838-3774 36pp.

Rutz, James "There's a New Church Coming" An orientation and preparation pamphlet for participants in a newly-open church. Tells the major benefits of an open church and how to take part in meetings. Contains most of the major insights found in *The Open Church.* Priced for mass distribution, a packet of ten is $6.00 plus $1.00 shipping from The SeedSowers. Inquire about quantity discounts: (207) 795-6615. 24 panels. Also available as a photocopiable master for $5.00 postpaid.

Shaw, Bobbi *The Open Church Study Guide*. Two study guides written for this book. One is a leader's manual and the other a guide for individuals. Books are three ring binders, which allow additional pages to be easily inserted. They are available directly from The SeedSowers, P.O. Box 3568, Beaumont, TX, 77704. (409) 838-3774. $9.95 plus $1.00 shipping.

Shelley, Bruce and Marshall *The Consumer Church*. A good illustration of the problems facing the church in the secular culture. The premise is that ministry is the responsibility and right of all Christians. Many stories used to make points. InterVarsity Press, Downers Grove, IL 60515 (1992) 256 pp.

Smith, Frank B. *Ultimate Evangelism*. Teaches repentance, prayer, discipleship, love and unity as it relates to the church and individuals. Published by Frank B. Smith, P.O. Box 3009, Vista, CA 92083 (1986) 142pp.

Snyder, Graydon *Church Life Before Constantine*. The only book in the English language on church archaeology. Blows to smithereens the traditional views of early church life. Available from The SeedSowers, P.O. Box 3568, Beaumont, TX, 77704 (409) 838-3774

Stedman, Ray C. *Body Life*. The classic book on sharing. Regal Books, Ventura, CA 93006 (1972) 182pp.

Stevens, Paul R. *Liberating the Laity: Equipping all the saints for ministry*. An outstanding book by a Canadian pastor who actually lived out what he prescribes in his book. Refreshing and different. He has excellent ideas and stories of what did and didn't work. Highly recommended reading. InterVarsity Press, Downers Grove, IL 60515 (1985) 192 pp.

Strauch, Alexander *Biblical Eldership*. Presented to restore Biblical leadership to the church. Available in a study guide, book, and short booklet. Lewis and Roth Publishers, Littleton, CO (1988) 288pp.

Tillapaugh, Frank R. *Unleashing The Church*. Great ideas and examples of programs that worked for a large Colorado church. Regal Books (1982) 224pp.

Trudinger, Ron *Cells For Life*. Reading on home groups as they relate to strengthening the church. King's Way Publications, Limited (1984) 123pp.

If you know of any other exciting books that relate to the open church movement, you're invited to send them to us (non-returnable) for review and possible inclusion in the next edition. Send your favorite books to:

Bobbi Shaw
Book Reviews
Open Church Ministries
P.O. Box 38519
Colorado Springs, CO 80937
(719) 471-9191
Fax: (719) 471-9488

Index